HIKE
YOSEMITE

Hike. Contemplate what makes you happy and what makes you happier still. Follow a trail or blaze a new one. **Hike.** Think about what you can do to expand your life and someone else's. **Hike.** Slow down. Gear up. **Hike.** Connect with friends. Re-connect with nature.

Hike. Shed stress. Feel blessed. **Hike** to remember. **Hike** to forget. **Hike** for recovery. **Hike** for discovery. **Hike.** Enjoy the beauty of providence. **Hike.** Share the way, The Hiker's Way, on the long and winding trail we call life.

HIKE YOSEMITE

BY
JOHN MCKINNEY

TheTrailmaster.com

HIKE Yosemite By John McKinney

HIKE Yosemite ©2022 The Trailmaster, Inc. All rights reserved. Manufactured in the United States of America. No part of this book may be used or reproduced in any manner whatsoever without written permission except in the case of brief quotations embodied in articles and reviews.

Acknowledgments: Many thanks to Mark Fincher, Wilderness Specialist, and to the Yosemite National Park staff, who have been unfailingly courteous and helpful to the author in the field and from the office.

ISBN: 978-0934161-88-6
Book Design by Lisa DeSpain
Cartography by Tom Harrison (TomHarrisonMaps.com)
HIKE Series Editor: Cheri Rae

Published by Olympus Press and The Trailmaster, Inc. www.TheTrailmaster.com (Visit our site for a complete listing of all Trailmaster publications, products, and services.)

Although The Trailmaster, Inc. and the author have made every attempt to ensure that information in this book is accurate, they are not responsible for any loss, damage, injury, or inconvenience that may occur to you while using this information. You are responsible for your own safety; the fact that an activity or trail is described in this book does not mean it will be safe for you. Trail conditions can change from day to day; always check local conditions and know your limitations.

Contents

INTRODUCTION 7

YOSEMITE NATIONAL PARK 13
    Geography, Natural Attractions, History,
    Administration

South Entrance

MARIPOSA GROVE 19
    These magnificent sequoias inspired creation of the
    national park

WAWONA MEADOW 23
    Lovely meadow circled by a rare year-round trail

SENTINEL DOME 25
    Small elevation gain yields far-reaching vistas

FROM GLACIER POINT 27
    Wonderful one-way sojourn down Panorama Trail to
    Yosemite Valley

Yosemite Valley

TO GLACIER POINT 31
    Classic Four Mile Trail ascends to the point from
    Yosemite Valley

VERNAL FALL 35
    Vernal and Nevada falls from Mist Trail and John Muir Trail

HALF DOME 39
    A long pilgrimage to Yosemite's icon summit

MIRROR LAKE 43
    Reflections of a changing environment

YOSEMITE VALLEY LOOP 47
    Heart of the valley walkabout with vistas of its most famed attractions

YOSEMITE FALLS 53
    Ascend in awe to the top of North America's highest waterfall

Big Oak Flat Entrance

TUOLUMNE GROVE 57
    Visit some of the largest living things and Dead Giant, too

MERCED GROVE 59
    Discover Yosemite's smallest and most remote sequoia grove

HETCH HETCHY 63
    Even flooded, this valley is something to behold

Tioga Pass Road

NORTH DOME 67
    Some hikers claim the dome provides the park's best panorama

Clouds Rest 71
  Climb to where the clouds rest, Yosemite's largest granite face

Tenaya Lake 75
  A real looker that must not be overlooked

Cathedral Lakes 77
  A sanctuary of lakes and the lofty spires of Cathedral Peak

Tuolumne Meadows 81
  Largest and most famous subalpine meadow in the High Sierra

Tuolumne Falls 85
  Mesmerizing passage along the Tuolumne River to a remote cascade

Lembert Dome 89
  Looks impossible to climb, but a trail leads to the great granite summit

Mono Pass 93
  Historic trail, historic pass, stirring eastern Sierra vistas

Gaylor Lakes 97
  From Yosemite's highest trailhead to two lakes and the Great Sierra Mine

Mt. Dana 101
  A climb to remember to the top of Yosemite's second-highest peak

Yosemite Stories 114

California's National Parks 130

About the Author 142

*Reflections on Yosemite:
Everything a national park should be and more.*

EVERY TRAIL TELLS A STORY.

Introduction

Famous for its great granite cliffs and domes, enormous waterfalls and giant sequoias, Yosemite is everything a national park should be and more. I love hiking here and so do hikers, experienced and not, from across the nation and around the world.

Such well-known Yosemite Valley destinations as Vernal Fall, Nevada Fall, Yosemite Falls and Half Dome are magnets for hikers. Equally attractive are many more sights outside the valley: Tuolumne Meadows, Cathedral Peak, Clouds Rest, the Mariposa Grove of Big Trees and many more.

The park boasts a magnificent High Sierra backcountry, one that (by rather severe Sierra standards anyway) is quite accessible. Well-marked trails lead to wildflower-festooned alpine meadows, lovely lakes and tarns, as well as to the tops of domes and peaks.

Four million visitors to the national park is a lot of people no matter how you look at it, though efforts to reduce auto traffic in the valley by extensive use of buses have been at least partially successful.

Unlike the motorist, diner or souvenir shopper, the hiker feels fewer effects of Yosemite's crowds. With the exception of the heavily trafficked "waterfall trails" and a couple other valley footpaths, the hiker is far less likely to feel the impact of such crowding and may even be surprised at achieving a measure of solitude. While Yosemite has 350 miles of roads, hikers will be pleased to know the national park also boasts 800 miles of hiking trails—many leading into remote wilderness.

Because of the extreme human and vehicle traffic conditions, two generations of so-called hiking authorities have repeated two words of advice about the floor of Yosemite Valley: "Stay away."

I disagree.

Considering the crowds and congestion that often overwhelm Yosemite Village and its asphalt arteries, the valley's trail system offers a surprisingly, and refreshingly, natural experience. To be sure Yosemite's heart-of-the-valley trails are very well used; however, they're not overwhelmed by hikers. And you just might find that traveling in company with hikers from many states and from halfway around the world is a unique experience, too.

Kids of all ages enjoy riding the shuttle bus just because it's a bus and because it puts most of Yosemite Valley's sights within easy hiking distance. Check out Yosemite Falls and El Capitan, pause for a picnic

Introduction

along the Merced River, hike a mile or two or three, then stop and ride the bus to conveniently located kid-friendly concessions such as a pizza place and ice cream parlor.

So let's acknowledge that Yosemite Valley has a lot of visitor amenities. And at the same time, let's be clear that Yosemite is a national park, not a theme park, and needs to be approached with a healthy respect for nature and fast-changing natural conditions.

One summer day in 2011 three hikers stepped past the guardrail at the top of Vernal Fall and were swept to their deaths. Coincidentally, I had hiked to Vernal Fall with my family just the day before.

Not long after the incident was reported, "John McKinney, Hiking Expert" was asked to comment on the tragedy for ABC World News. I said, in part: "My heart goes out to the families of the hikers and to the horrified onlookers. At the same time, my head cannot comprehend the decision-making that occurred when the hikers decided to step into the raging Merced River at the top of Vernal Fall."

Please use common sense, obey natural laws and heed park regulations. With the right preparations and precautions, a hike in Yosemite can be a memorable experience—for all the right reasons.

Some Yosemite Valley trails are accessible all year. While the park has glaciated peaks that rise to more than 13,000 feet in elevation, Yosemite Valley is less than a mile high and some park areas are even below 3,000 feet. In spring, Yosemite's waterfalls are at their most majestic. In summer, alpine slopes burst into bloom. Autumn is a favorite time for a hike when the "Range of Light" is particularly dramatic and the aspens glow like fire in the wind.

John Muir's suggested hikes in his 1912 Yosemite guidebook were 25 miles long. One can only imagine hikers of that era were of sturdier stock—or perhaps few followed in Muir's footsteps.

My suggested hikes in this modern-day Yosemite guidebook are a wee bit (in fact, mostly a lot) shorter than those detailed by John Muir; nevertheless they are Yosemite classics all and some will keep the average hiker on the trail for an entire day.

My selection of hikes was a difficult task indeed because I had to choose among dozens of favorites—each a wonderful hike in its own right. Hikes detailed in this book represent a range of difficulty levels and a variety of locations—from Yosemite Valley to Glacier Point to Tuloumne Meadows.

Each trail tells a different story. The trail up Mt. Dana was constructed at the behest of esteemed Yosemite botanist Dr. Carl Sharsmith who designed a route that minimized human impact on the mountain's fragile flora. Yosemite Falls Trail, like some other early (1870s) paths, was privately built and operated as a toll trail. Mirror Lake was once auto-accessible; now the road to the lake is a walking path.

At any moment on any hike in Yosemite National Park you might just notice what nature writer Joseph Smeaton Chase, author of the early 20th century classic, *Yosemite Trails*, called "the thousand and one things that make up the silent conversation of the trail."

Yosemite's trails are for the most part well engineered, well maintained and well signed. Because of the park's attraction to visitors worldwide, the park service uses lots of international symbols on its signage, and the metric system as well. Interpretive information and safety advice is printed and posted in many languages.

Opportunities for summer solitude may be limited on the major trails, but the farther away from a road one hikes, the greater the opportunity for tranquility. "Well-used" is a better characterization of most Yosemite trails than "overused." The journey on these pathways is often as pleasurable as the famed destinations they reach.

Hike smart, reconnect with nature and have a wonderful time on the trail.

Hike on.

John McKinney

El Capitan, Yosemite's iconic granite monolith, attracts rock-climbers from around the world.

EVERY TRAIL TELLS A STORY.

YOSEMITE NATIONAL PARK

Geography

Located in the central part of the Sierra Nevada, 1,189 square mile Yosemite National Park sprawls over three counties—Tuolumne, Mariposa and Madera—and is surrounded by three wilderness areas—Ansel Adams, Hoover and Emigrant. The park includes scores of lakes as well two major rivers—the Merced and Tuolumne—both of which begin in Yosemite and have "Wild and Scenic River" status.

John Muir's pioneering work in glacial theory first helped us understand that Yosemite Valley was mainly created into its U-shape by glaciers. Glaciers began altering the uplifted rock of the High Sierra some 2 to 3 million years ago and continued sculpting Yosemite until about 10 thousand years ago. Those steep granite walls account for Yosemite's many spectacular waterfalls.

Park elevations range widely from Yosemite Valley at about 4,000 feet to 9,941-foot Tioga Pass, highest mountain pass in California. Many Yosemite peaks top 10,000 feet. Mt. Lyell (13,114 feet) is Yosemite's highest peak with Mt. Dana (13,057 feet) a close second.

Natural Attractions

Most discussions of the national park's attractions begin with its spectacular waterfalls, including Yosemite Falls, at 2,425 feet, highest waterfall in North America and third highest on the planet. Vernal Fall and Nevada Fall, cascades of uncommon beauty, can be visited via the wondrous Mist Trail and famed John Muir Trail. The park is also known for its groves of giant sequoia. Grizzly Giant, patriarch of Mariposa Grove, is estimated to have sprouted some 2,700 years ago.

A wide range of elevations (from 3,000 to 13,000 feet) accounts for a diversity of ecological communities, including oak woodland, mixed conifer forest and meadows (Tuolumne Meadows is the largest High Sierra meadow), plus that very special environment above timberline. White Mariposa lily, corn lily, paint brush, shooting stars, the showy, bright red snowplant—Yosemite's wildflowers are abundant and include lots of varieties of lupine and more than 30 species of monkeyflowers. Yosemite was designated as a UNESCO World Heritage Site in 1984 because of its geology, biodiversity and history.

Mammals, large and small, include black bears, mountain lions, mule deer, marmots, porcupine and pika. Yosemite has exceptional bird diversity, with 262 species including the American dipper, John Muir's favorite bird.

History

The magnificent sequoias of Mariposa Grove, along with the wondrous Yosemite Valley, prompted President Abraham Lincoln to set aside Yosemite as a reserve and grant it (temporarily) to the state of California for its protection in 1864. It's not exaggeration to say that this grove of giant sequoias inspired

Wouldn't you have liked to hike along with John Muir and President Theodore Roosevelt as they toured Yosemite together?!

the first steps toward the establishment of America's entire system of national parks.

John Muir is inextricably linked with Yosemite. The great naturalist's passionate efforts to make Yosemite a park have long been admired and will be appreciated by generations to come. Tourism grew rapidly and at the dawn of the 20th century Muir and the Sierra Club began urging the federal government to make Yosemite a national park like Yellowstone, the nation's first. President Theodore Roosevelt toured the park with Muir, and placed Yosemite under federal protection in 1906. In 1916 the National Park Service was founded and Yosemite immediately placed under the new agency's protection. Tioga Pass Road and many campgrounds were constructed and tourism to Yosemite greatly increased.

Administration

The National Park Service has stewardship for the 748,542 acres of Yosemite National Park. The iconic park is particularly challenging to manage because it attracts huge numbers of visitors from around the world and because the agency's mission requires it to protect park features and its many ecological communities. About 95 percent of the park is wilderness and must be managed accordingly.

If you're planning a visit to Yosemite National Park, you can get general information on accommodations, weather, and permits from the park's touchtone phone menu at 209-372-0200 or online at www.nps.gov/yose. The hearing-impaired can get information by calling 209-372-4726. For camping reservations, call 877-444-6777 or visit www.recreation.gov.

In the park, the biggest visitor center is the Valley Visitor Center in Yosemite Village 209-372-0200, which provides all sorts of information and offers daily ranger programs.

You can buy books and maps from the nonprofit Yosemite Association, 209-379-2646; www.yosemite.org. For information on much of the lodging within Yosemite National Park, contact travelyosemite.com, the site of the authorized concessionaire, Yosemite Hospitality LLC, a subsidiary of Aramark.

Yosemite's flattest trail circles Wawona Meadows, festooned with wildflowers in the spring.

EVERY TRAIL TELLS A STORY.

I
SOUTH ENTRANCE

HIKE ON.

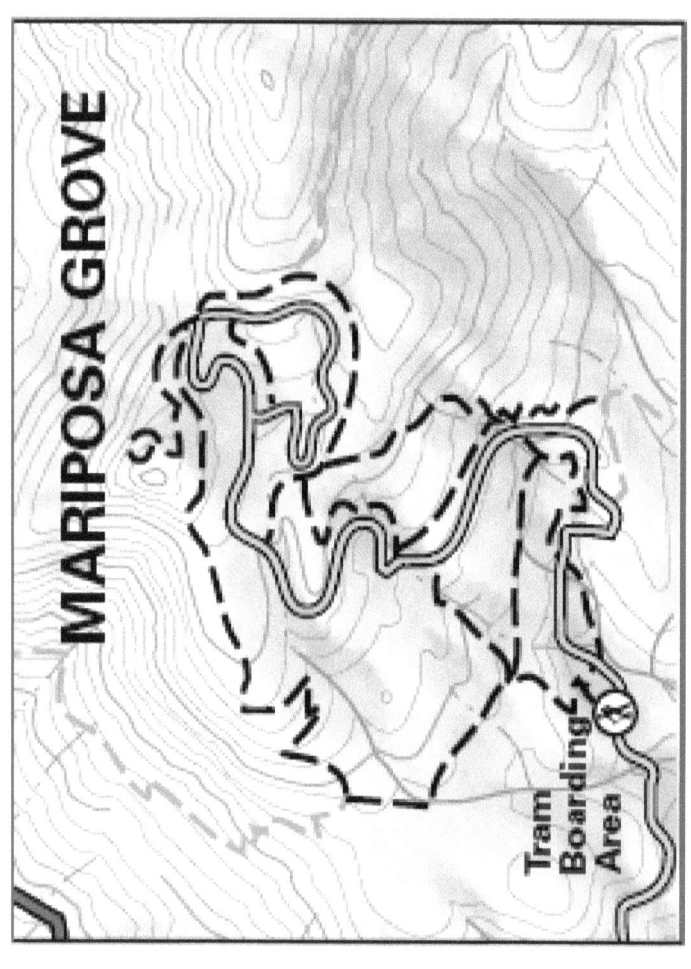

Mariposa Grove

Mariposa Grove Trail

To Grizzly Giant is 1.6 miles round trip with 100-foot elevation gain; or 4.8-mile loop with 1,000-foot elevation gain

Mariposa is by far the largest of Yosemite's three groves of giant sequoias and the one that inspired the creation of the national park. See Grizzly Giant, the Three Graces, California Tunnel Tree and many more outstanding big trees.

Likely you will have lots of company on your walk among the world's largest living things. The enormous trees—combined with easy access, close proximity to the park's south entrance, a gift/snack shop, and a narrated open-air tram tour no less—really draw a crowd.

DIRECTIONS: From Highway 41 at Yosemite's South Entrance Station, drive east two miles to Mariposa Grove. The huge parking lot can fill up by 10 a.m. on a busy summer morning. When the lot is full, NPS stops entries and provides free shuttle service from Highway 41.

THE HIKE: Pick up a copy of the park service's "Mariposa Grove of Giant Sequoias" pamphlet (available in several languages) from the dispenser and begin walking the gentle path.

You'll soon arrive at Fallen Monarch, which came to the nation's attention in 1899 via a widely circulated photo of U.S. Calvary officers (with their horses!) posed atop the horizontal tree. Cross the road, ascend some steps, and cross the road again.

The path leads to Three Graces, with roots so intertwined that should one tree fall, the other two would topple as well. Apart from the three is a more solitary sequoia dubbed The Bachelor.

Next visit Grizzly Giant, grove patriarch, blackened, scarred and estimated to have sprouted 2,700 years ago; it's likely the oldest sequoia in Mariposa Grove. For most visitors, the famed tree is the unofficial "tourist turnaround."

Not far from Grizzly Giant is California Tunnel Tree. No nineteenth century visit was complete without a stage ride through a tree with a tunnel in its midsection. It's hike-through not drive-through these days.

Onward on Upper (or Outer) Loop Trail to the Faithful Couple, two large trees fused together for 50 feet or so along their lower trunks, but separated above. Inspect wildfire-bisected Clothespin Tree meet the tram road, and join Museum Trail. Descend to

Grove Museum and learn more about sequoia ecology and history. The museum is located on the site of Yosemite guardian Galen Clark's 1864 cabin.

The tree tour continues with the curious Telescope Tree; look up the trunk to see the sky. Thousands of wagons, then cars drove through Wawona Tunnel Tree, from 1881, when a tunnel was bored through it, until the big winter of 1968-9 when it fell. The path curves west to visit Galen Clark Tree, honoring the Yosemite pioneer and discoverer of Mariposa Grove.

Return to the trailhead via the sequoias by backtracking to the museum and descending to the parking lot. Or take Outer Loop Trail, which travels out of the sequoias into a lovely mixed forest of incense cedar, sugar pine and white fir, and circles back.

Mariposa Grove: No wonder it was the inspiration for creation of Yosemite National Park.

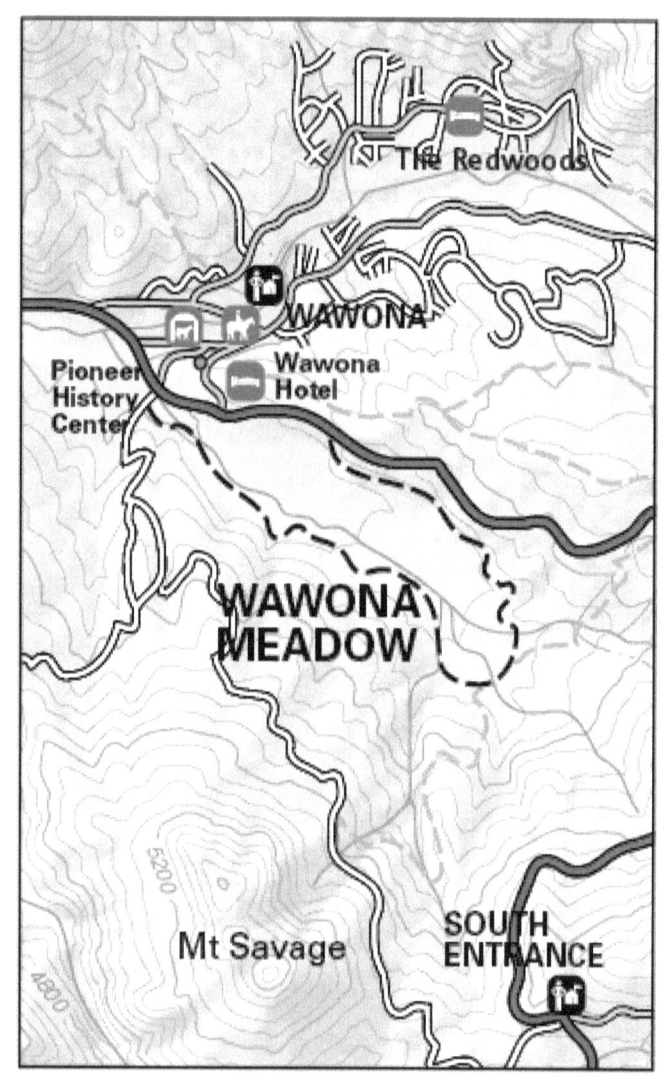

TheTrailmaster.com

Wawona Meadow
Meadow Trail

3-mile loop

Near the lovely Wawona Hotel, Yosemite's flattest trail (with rare year-round access) circles family-friendly Wawona Meadow, a delight in spring and early summer when wildflowers color the meadow. Deer frequently can be seen browsing the meadow.

DIRECTIONS: From Yosemite's South Entrance, follow Highway 41 north 7 miles to the Wawona Hotel. The signed path begins across the highway from the hotel parking lot.

THE HIKE: Angle across the golf course and meander south on a gentle ascent on the pine needle-strewn road in the company of oaks, pines and cedars. Enjoy an equally gentle descent along the east side of the meadow. The looping pathway returns you to Highway 41 near Wawona Hotel.

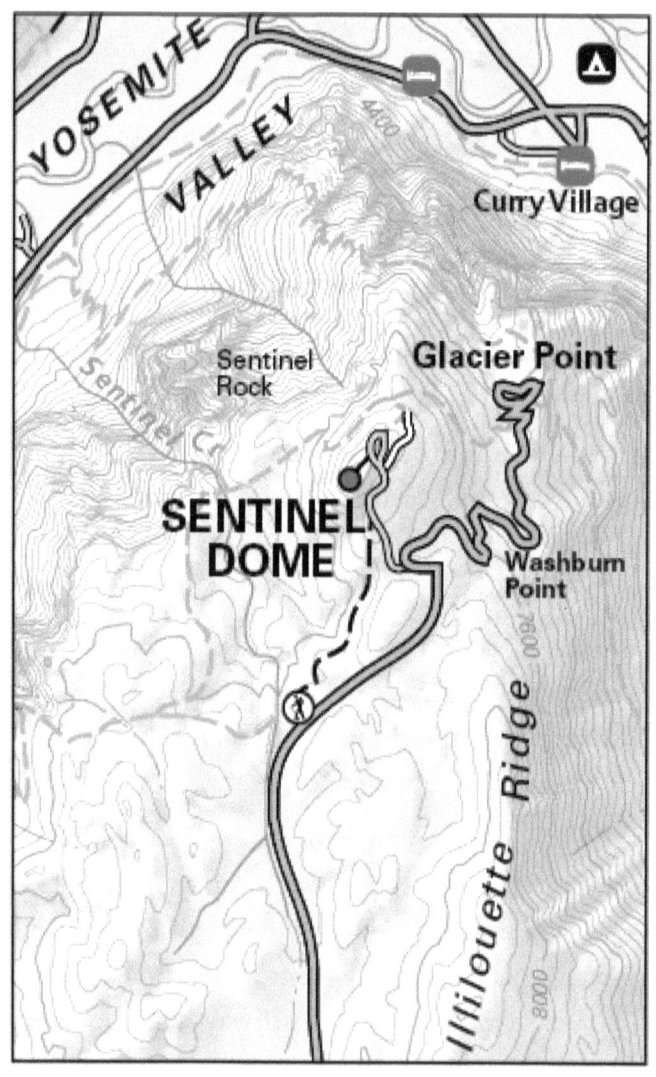

Sentinel Dome

Sentinel Dome Trail

To Sentinel Dome is 2.2 miles round trip with 400-foot elevation gain

Rarely does a hiker get so grand a view for so little gain and pain. Some hikers claim the view from the top of 8,122-foot Sentinel Dome is better than the one from Glacier Point.

DIRECTIONS: From Highway 41 at Chinquapin, follow Glacier Point Road 13 miles to a parking area, 2 miles from Glacier Point.

THE HIKE: Begin a mellow ascent over open granite slopes, pass through a pine and white fir forest and intersect an old road. The wide path ascends from forest to exposed granite and passes a junction with trails that lead to Glacier Point and Yosemite Valley. No pathway climbs Sentinel Dome but the route up its wide backside is quite apparent.

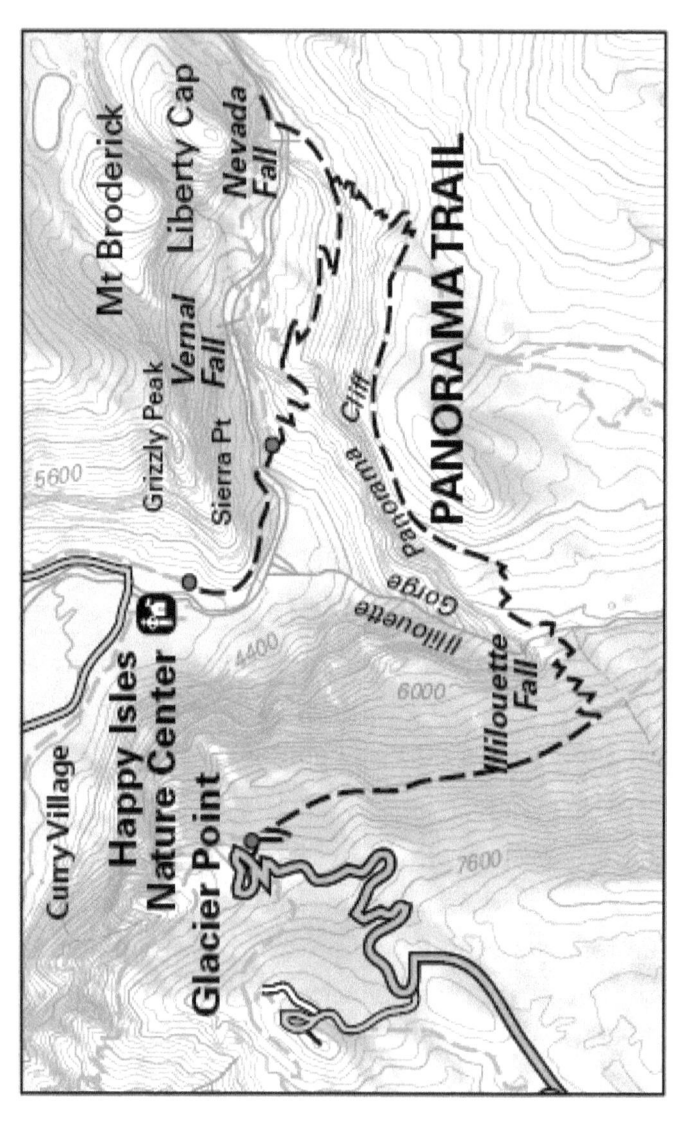

TheTrailmaster.com

From Glacier Point

Glacier Point-Panorama, John Muir Trails

From Glacier Point to Valley Floor is 9 miles one way with 3,200-foot elevation loss

Panorama Trail delivers the promise in its name: fabulous views of Half Dome, Liberty Cap and Clouds Rest. Each turn in the trail brings the hikers another dramatic vista. Even Yosemite icons Vernal and Nevada falls, so difficult to glimpse simultaneously from the valley floor, can be seen in a new light—together—from Panorama Trail.

These super views make this hike the park's best one-way trip down to Yosemite Valley's Happy Isles. A car shuttle is necessary or, better yet, board one of the regularly scheduled buses to Glacier Point.

Glacier Point was the launch pad for Yosemite's after-dark, crowd-pleasing Firefall. Piles of burning embers were pushed over the edge to create a spectacle that was popular for nearly a hundred years before it was halted in 1968.

While your descent to Yosemite Valley may not be as dramatic as the Firefall, it will be one to remember. On the way to Happy Isles you'll get a great at-the-brink view of Illilouette Fall, visit Nevada and Vernal falls, and travel the historic John Muir Trail.

DIRECTIONS: Follow Glacier Point Road all the way (16 miles) to its end at Glacier Point. The signed path begins at the east end of the parking area.

Glacier Point Road, which provides the only access by car to the point, usually opens around late May or early June, and closes in late October/early November depending on conditions. A tour bus bound for Glacier Point departs three times daily (8:30a.m., 10a.m. and 1:30p.m.) from Yosemite Lodge at the Falls. This tour operates from late spring to early fall, conditions permitting. Hikers wishing to catch a ride up and hike down to Yosemite Valley can purchase one-way tickets to Glacier Point.

THE HIKE: After a brief climb, the trail forks—Pohono Trail to the right and our Panorama-Glacier Point Trail to the left. Descend among red fir, blackened but not killed by a 1987 wildfire, enjoying the first of the panoramic views between singed trunks.

At 1.7 mile, the path passes a junction with Buena Vista Trail and soon offers a short connector trail leading to a viewpoint for Illilouette Fall. After another quarter-mile descent the path leads over a bridge over Illilouette Creek, then ascends Panorama Cliff above the fall. With the climb come more fabulous views, including a heart-stopper from Panorama Point.

The trail begins a mellow descent, leveling out as it heads eastward to a junction with Mono Meadow Trail. A mile-long switchbacking descent through the forest brings you to a junction with John Muir Trail. Continue a bit farther for an eye-popping look to the brink of Nevada Fall, then return to the JMT for the hike to Vernal Fall. (See Vernal and Nevada falls hike description.)

After crossing the Merced River on a bridge, the John Muir Trail delivers you to Happy Isles. Walk or take the shuttle bus to Curry Village.

It's all downhill from here to the Valley floor.

In Yosemite Valley, mule deer are especially common, seen browsing on leaves, grass, and herbs.

EVERY TRAIL TELLS A STORY.

II
YOSEMITE VALLEY

HIKE ON.

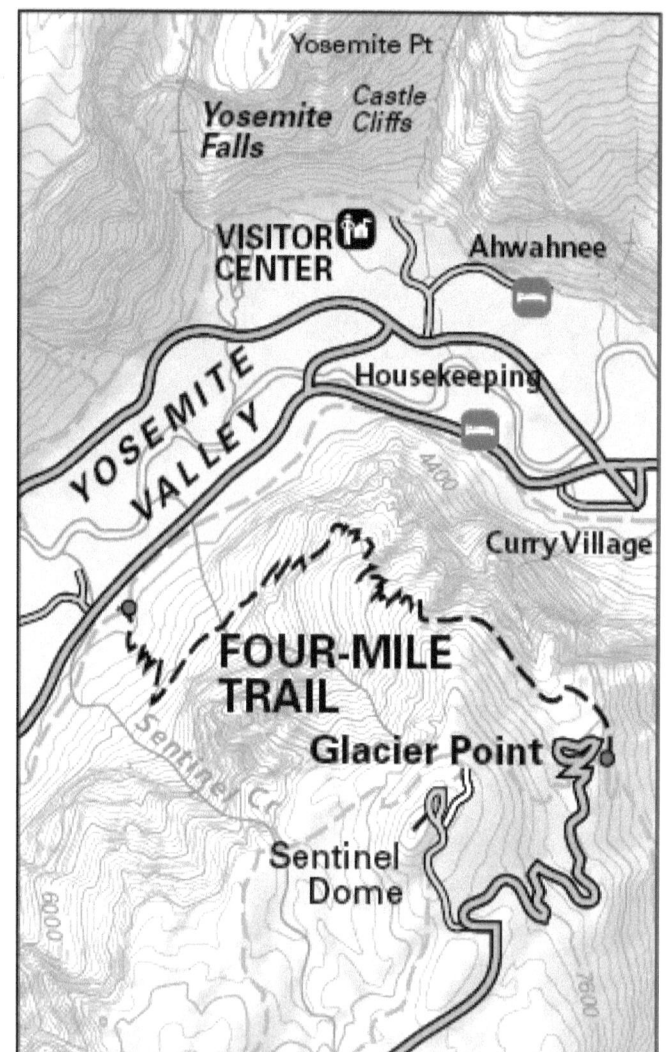

TheTrailmaster.com

TO GLACIER POINT

FOUR-MILE TRAIL

To Glacier Point is 9.2 miles round trip with 3,200-foot elevation gain

Four-Mile Trail is a Yosemite classic, the original route to Glacier Point. With the climb comes panoramic views (quite different perspective from the usual postcard ones) beginning with the meandering Merced River, then Upper Yosemite Falls, El Capitan, Half Dome, Vernal Fall and much, much more.

Hotelier James McCauley hired John Conway to construct a trail from Yosemite Valley to Glacier Point. Hikers paid a $1 toll to trek the trail. When first constructed in the 1872, the path extended 4 miles, but after an overhaul in the 1920s and the addition of switchbacks it now measures 4.6 miles. No matter, the original trail name is still with us.

From Four-Mile Trail, Yosemite Falls is revealed to the hiker in all its glory. Elsewhere in Yosemite Valley, the view of the falls is just a bit impeded by trees or rocks, but from the path you'll enjoy a direct view of the cascade.

DIRECTIONS: The signed trailhead and pull-outs for parking are located along Southside Drive in Yosemite Valley, 1.2 miles west of Yosemite Village. To reach Glacier Point, head out of the valley about 9 miles south on Highway 41, then follow Glacier Point Road 16 miles east to the parking lot and trailhead.

Glacier Point Road, offering the only access by car to the point and upper trailhead for the Four-Mile Trail, usually opens around late May or early June, and closes in late October/early November depending on conditions. A tour bus bound for Glacier Point departs three times daily from Yosemite Lodge at the Falls. Hikers wishing to catch a ride up and hike down to Yosemite Valley can purchase one-way tickets to Glacier Point.

THE HIKE: As if to disguise its charms, the first 25 percent of Four-Mile Trail is simply a mellow meander across the valley floor followed by a moderate ascent among oak and manzanita. For we impatient hikers, it seems to take a long time to leave traffic noises behind. More patient sojourners will admire the mossy rocks and splashes of wildflowers in the spring.

About 1.5 miles out, the real climb begins—first through more oak woodland then among incense cedar and white fir. It's about 2.3 miles of very steep ascent, rewarded by ever-more expansive vistas of

Yosemite Valley and ever-more lofty views of Yosemite Falls until you reach a point where you're actually looking down at the famed falls.

Trail Gate, a bit more than three miles from the trailhead is just that: a gate across the trail that's closed in winter to stop hikers from hiking to Glacier Point. Even sans gate, it would not be sensible to hike snow-slippery slopes in winter.

The trail passes under Sentinel Rock. Nearby is Sentinel Dome, a 8,122-foot promontory that some hikers claim provides better views than those from Glacier Point. Finally, you finish all those switchbacks and the last mile is a cooler, calmer climb and contour amidst sugar pine and white fir to Glacier Point.

Hikers appreciate the view all the more after completing the challenging ascent to Glacier Point from the valley floor.

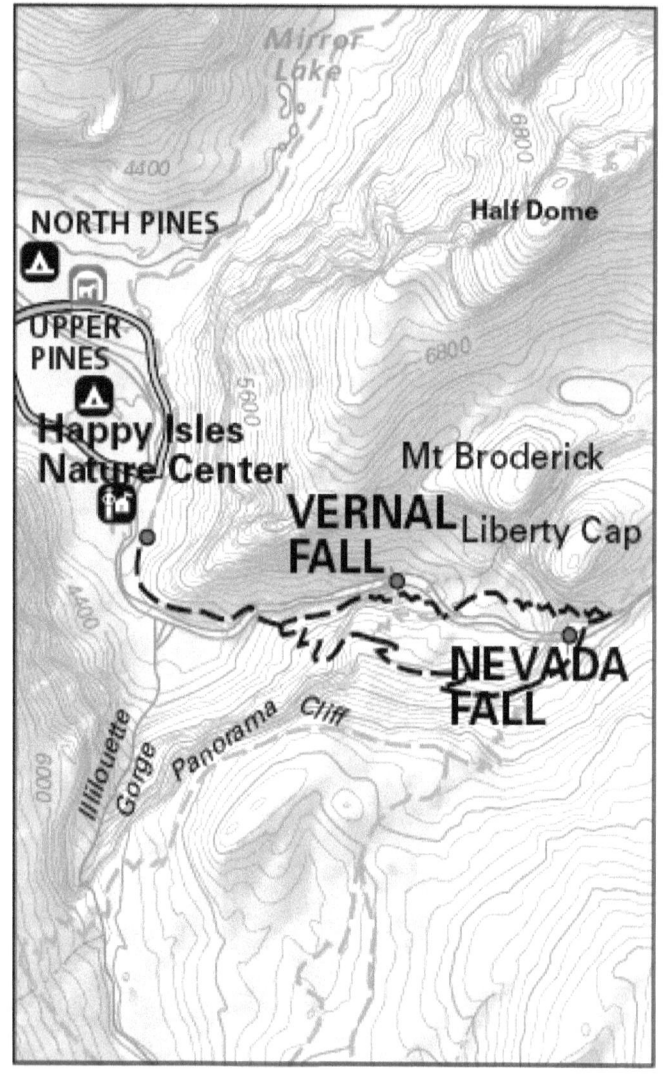

TheTrailmaster.com

Vernal Fall and Nevada Fall

Mist, John Muir Trails

To Vernal Fall is 3 miles round trip with 1,000-foot elevation gain; to Nevada Fall is 7 miles round trip with 2,000-foot gain

Two famous falls and two famous footpaths are highlights of this popular hike many consider Yosemite's most scenic. Vernal Fall is a cascade of uncommon beauty, a 317-foot Merced River spill that plunges over bold granite cliffs. Mist billows from the crashing water, rainbows arch toward the heavens.

Some say 594-foot Nevada Fall resembles an avalanche of snow. Magnificent Mist Trail and John Muir Trail get you there and back. Hikers short of time should at least make the 1.6-mile round trip pilgrimage to Vernal Fall Bridge.

DIRECTIONS: Park in the Curry Village day-use lot and take the shuttle bus to the stop for Happy Isles. If you take this hike during the off-season, you'll have to walk a mile from Curry Village to the trailhead.

THE HIKE: Join the wide paved pathway, soon crossing a bridge over the Merced River. Ascend amidst oak and bay, and reach Vernal Fall Bridge after 0.8 mile. Here you'll find toilets, drinking water and a fine view.

Climb onward, choose Mist Trail at a junction and ascend mist-slickened rock stairs. If the river is up, expect to get hosed by spray.

A guardrail adds a measure of security for hikers climbing the granite cliffs. Emerge from the mist, and if you're lucky see a rainbow superimposed over the spectacular scene. Tramp the balance of the trail to the top of the falls and a viewpoint. (Don't step past the guardrail; you will likely die, as several hikers did in 2011.)

After admiring Vernal Fall, walk up-river to Emerald Pool and Silver Apron, a beautiful, broad, river-washed rock formation that resembles a fan. (Do not step into the powerful currents; people die doing this.)

Cross a footbridge over the Merced, and curve briefly through the woods. The path isn't as steep as that to Vernal Fall, but plenty vertical! Nevada Fall, too, is quite the mist generator, but it sprays down-canyon not over the trail.

Tackle two dozen or so switchbacks, reach the top and a junction with the trail to Half Dome. To visit the fall and to return to the valley via John Muir Trail, descend 0.2 mile to the top of Nevada Fall. Flat rocks suggest a lunch stop. This is a superb top-down look at a waterfall because the rock lip of the overlook juts out and Nevada Fall's cascade is not precisely vertical.

Cross the Merced on a bridge, and begin your return to Happy Isles on the John Muir Trail, carefully negotiating slippery switchbacks. The path travels below well-named Panoramic Cliffs and serves up grand views back of Half Dome, Liberty Cap and Nevada Fall. Nearing the Merced again, you'll meet a bridle trail but stick with the footpath, bearing right to return to this hike's first junction with the Mist Trail. Bear left and retrace your steps to Vernal Fall Bridge and Happy Isles.

Mist Trail leads to the top of Vernal Fall. Watch your step!

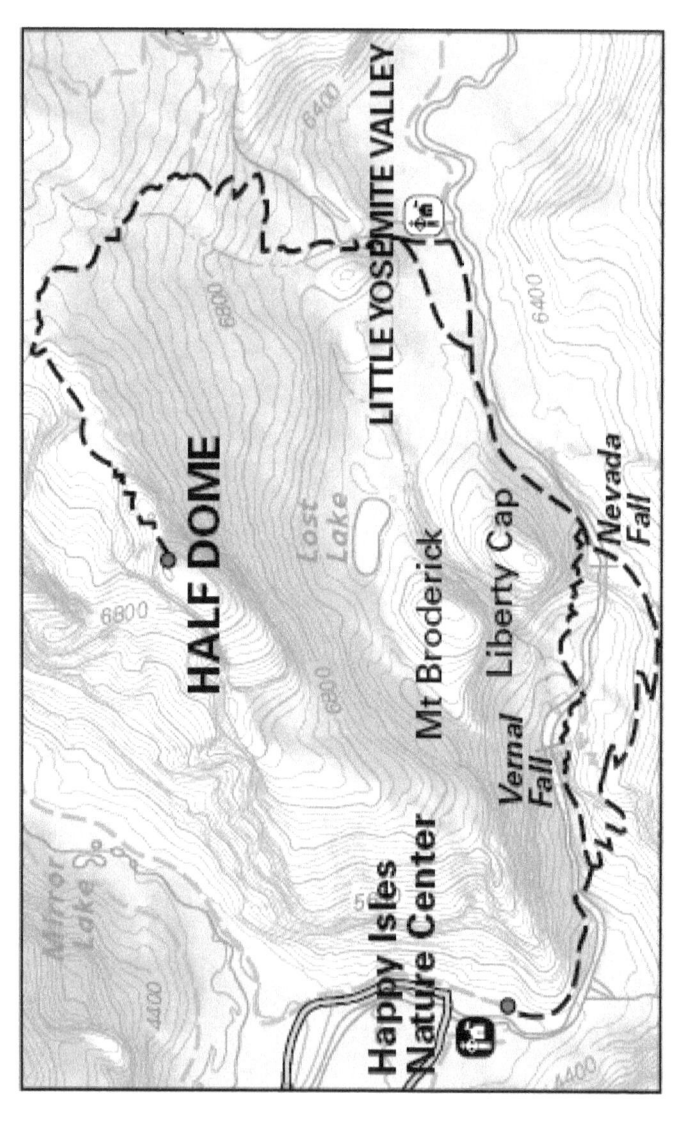

HALF DOME

MIST, JOHN MUIR, HALF DOME TRAILS

From Happy Isles to Half Dome summit is 16.5 miles round trip with 4,800-foot elevation gain (14.2 miles round trip via Mist Trail)

This long pilgrimage to Yosemite's icon summit definitely makes the once-in-a-lifetime list. From the 8,842-foot dome enjoy 360-degree vistas: Yosemite Valley, Clouds Rest and Cathedral Peak, the jagged Sierra crest.

Reaching the summit requires climbing at an almost 45-degree angle up slick granite with the help of twin cables that hikers grip to haul themselves to the top. Depending on weather conditions, the park service installs the cables in mid-May and removes them in early October. Bring gloves.

Permits are required to hike Half Dome and a quota system is in effect. To learn more and to apply for a permit, visit Recreation.gov or call 877-444-6777.

Get an early start because mid-afternoon summer thunderstorms are common. Last place you want to be in an electric storm is atop Half Dome, forced to make a hurried descent over slippery rock while holding on to wet metal cables.

DIRECTIONS: Park in the large lot at Curry Village. Take the shuttle bus to Happy Isles.

THE HIKE: (See Vernal Fall account in this guide.) After reaching Vernal Fall, choose between Mist Trail and John Muir Trail. Mist Trail shaves almost a mile from the distance, but is a strenuous, stair-stepping route. JMT ascends more moderately via well-engineered switchbacks—a better choice for travelers to Half Dome.)

Above Nevada Fall reach a junction with the trail to Half Dome. The path heads up-river, now a much more mellow Merced, slower and deeper than the one you've followed below the falls. A mile out from Nevada Fall, the trail splits. A slightly shorter bypass route forks left and passes near a restroom, but I suggest sticking with the trail leading to Little Yosemite Valley Camp, site of the last toilet on the way to Half Dome.

Leaving the camp behind, climb again (900 feet in elevation over the next 1.5 miles) to reach a junction, six miles from the start. Leave JMT and continue north on Half Dome Trail. In a half-mile, look eastward (right) for a short side trail to a spring, last water en route.

Now the granite grandeur unfolds: Half Dome on your left, Clouds Rest on your right. Warning signs remind you not to proceed to Half Dome in bad weather or if bad weather threatens.

About 0.75-mile from the top, begin the final ascent. Climb granite steps, top a minor dome and descend briefly to a saddle and the cables. (Caution, chipmunks! Don't leave behind daypacks with food in them.) Glove-up, get a grip on the cables (and yourself) and start climbing. Surmount a series of horizontal bars while gripping a pair of chains for the 400 feet of ascent over smooth granite.

Half Dome's highest point is located at the north end. Enjoy views of every major feature in Yosemite Valley and a panorama of peaks, but stay away from the cliff edge.

Put Half Dome on your once-in-a-lifetime hike list!

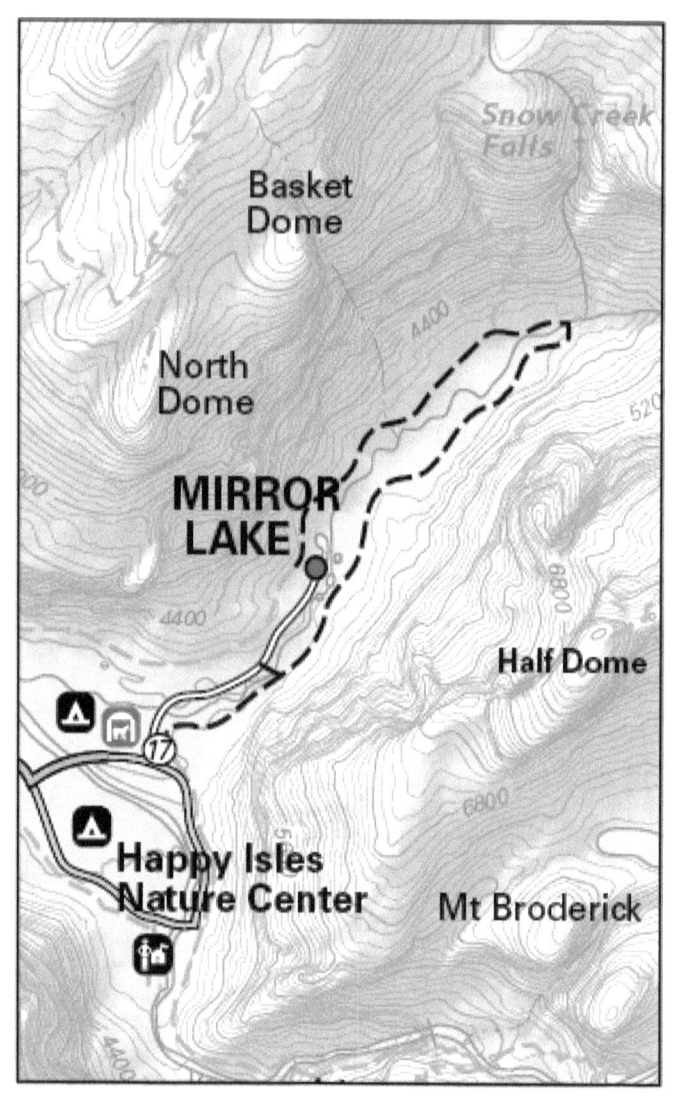

TheTrailmaster.com

Mirror Lake

Mirror Lake Trail

From Shuttle Bus Stop to Mirror Lake is 2 miles round trip; with optional Tenaya Creek loop is 4.8 miles round trip

Once upon a time, Half Dome's reflection in Mirror Lake was beautiful to behold, a living postcard admired by generations of Yosemite Valley visitors.

Such reflections are rare now, and will soon be no more.

Never a deep body of water, it was a pond naturally enclosed by a rockfall. In 1890, humans enhanced the little lake's reflective qualities by constructing a dam.

Mirror Lakes usually dries up at summer's end. In years past at this time the park service dredged the lakebed, hauling away tons of sand and gravel.

In 1971, this practice was stopped, and each year hence silt has accumulated to make Mirror Lake ever-smaller. These days Mirror is quite literally just a shadow of its former self, a gravely lake bottom fringed by a meadow with a branch of Tenaya Creek flowing through it.

Mellow Mirror Lake may be, but it's been subject to strong natural forces, too. Evidence of the great flood of 1997 is quite obvious in the area around the upper footbridge. Just downstream from the bridge, the trail passes through debris from the 2009 Ahwiyah Point Rockfall—one of the largest rockfalls in recent park history.

Mirror Meadow, er, lake, nevertheless remains a popular destination for day hikers. The setting, even without reflection, still inspires. Kids enjoy frolicking in and along Tenaya Creek.

The shuttle bus stops a mile from the lake and you may choose to walk the distance along a paved road or hoof it along a bridle trail. Beyond the lake, you may extend your walk by tramping up and down the narrow canyon cut by Tenaya Creek. The extra distance rewards with a bit of forested solitude.

DIRECTIONS: Take the Yosemite Valley shuttle bus to stop #17, Mirror Lake.

THE HIKE: Saunter (usually with lots of company) along the paved road, soon crossing Tenaya Creek on a stone bridge. The road winds with the river, climbing gently to Mirror Lake.

At the bridge you can lose some of the crowd by joining the dirt bridle trail that travels through a very mixed forest of oak, Douglas fir, incense cedar and big-leaf maple to the lake. Despite the guided platoons of rental horses (stand aside to let them pass) and plethora of road apples, the bridle trail is an enjoyable and altogether a more peaceful walk than the paved route.

Once at the lake, such as it is, locate the bridle trail on the north side and begin walking on a meandering trail that leads away from the lake.

Travel amidst forest and ferns, pass a junction with the trail leading to Tenaya Lake, and reach a wooden bridge that spans frisky Tenaya Creek. Now follow the Bridle Trail along the south side of the creek. Look up from the nearly level trail to admire Basket Dome and Half Dome. Continue past Mirror Lake 0.25 mile, cross Tenaya Creek on a footbridge, and rejoin the paved road leading back to the shuttle bus stop.

In the best of times, Mirror Lake lives up to the promise of its name.

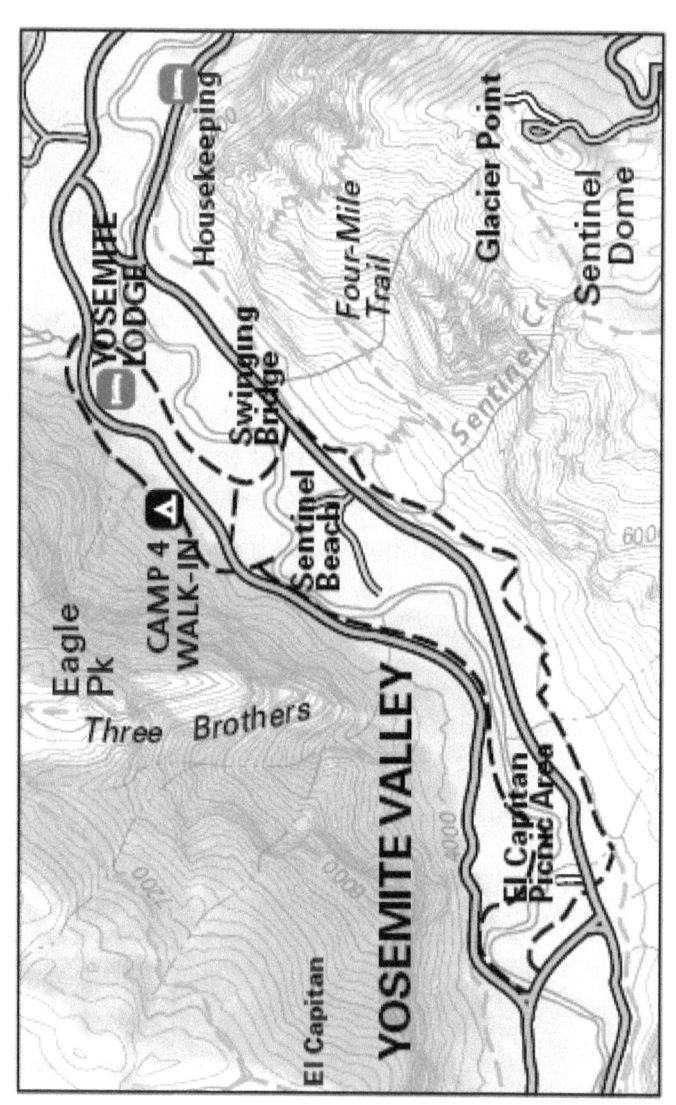

TheTrailmaster.com

Yosemite Valley

Valley Trails

5.5-mile loop

The tram tour of Yosemite Valley is fine, but to really appreciate the valley, hit the trail. On this heart of the valley walkabout, you'll enjoy vistas of many of its most famed attractions.

Veteran valley hikers all have their favorite loops: long and short, Village Loop or Lodge Loop. Hiking options are limited only by the finite number of bridges over the Merced River.

This is The Trailmaster's favorite middle-distance Yosemite Valley jaunt. Lengthen the described loop by continuing west to Bridalveil Meadow and Bridalveil Fall or by meandering east via the network of paths connecting The Ahwanee, Curry Village and Yosemite Village.

In spring, segments of the trail can be underwater. Be careful walking along Northside Drive.

DIRECTIONS: Day-use parking is available at Yosemite Lodge at the Falls. Or take the valley shuttle bus to stop #8 right in front of the lodge. Walk to the eastern end of the lodge complex and parking area and curve up to Northside Drive.

THE HIKE: Cross Northside Drive to meet the east-west trending footpath near its junction with Lower Yosemite Fall Trail and hike west (left) on the path. The wide path soon leads to the major Yosemite Falls trailhead and the wide paths that lead to the falls. Enjoy vistas of the three-tiered wonder as you continue southwest to the busy parking lot of Camp 4.

Camp 4, by far the least expensive place to sleep in the park, attracts at least four kinds of visitors: Europeans (mostly young), Americans (mostly young), budget travelers of all ages and rock climbers.

Some of the best rock climbers in the world came to the valley to challenge Yosemite's walls in the years after World War II. They gathered at Camp 4 to share their ideas about routes and gear.

Follow the path southwest through camp and surrounding woodland to Northside Drive. A crosswalk beckons you to cross the road and check out Leidig Meadow. The meadow, named for hoteliers Isabella and George Leidig who constructed an inn situated below Sentinel Rock in 1869, offers grand views of Half Dome, Clouds Rest and much more.

Meander gentle trails around Yosemite Valley and behold the postcard panoramas of towering peaks and magnificent waterfalls.

After admiring the meadow, double-back across Northside Drive and continue on the path a short distance to the actual crossing of the road and a trail sign indicating it's 2.3 miles to El Capitan and 5.9 miles to Bridalveil Fall.

The path meanders between Northside Road and the willow- and cottonwood-cloaked north bank of the Merced River. Cross Northside Road to El Capitan Picnic Area or pick your own picnic spot along the Merced.

While hikers can't help spending a lot of time looking up at the majestic walls of the valley, the valley floor is worth a close look as well. Yellow pine forest is the dominant environment, though tree-lovers will find other pines, including Ponderosa, lodgepole and sugar, as well as oaks, willows and dogwood. The valley's large meadows are seasonally sprinkled with such wildflowers as Chinese Houses, California poppy, Western buttercup, Indian pink and star flower.

Continue another 0.5 mile west along the Merced to Devil's Elbow, which doesn't sound named for fun, but actually is kind of Yosemite's Riviera—a sandy beach with plenty of flat rocks for sunbathing. The view of El Capitan from Devil's Elbow was one of the great photographer Ansel Adams' favorites.

Cross the river via the road over El Capitan Bridge, a great place from which to observe mighty El Capitan, towering 3,593 feet above the Merced River. Rock climbers are frequently seen ascending the monolith, one of the largest blocks of exposed granite in the world.

From the bridge, pick up the signed bridle path ("Curry Village 4.1 miles") heading southeast. Admire the Cathedral Rocks and Cathedral Spires on the eastern side of the valley; some hikers think these rocks are as impressive as El Capitan. One of the most famous works of art inspired by Yosemite, *Cathedral Rocks, Yosemite Valley, Winter*, was created in 1872 by the renowned landscape painter Albert Bierstadt.

Cross Southside Drive, head briefly south, then east, on a two-mile stretch of trail in the shadow of the valley's south wall. Savor magnificent views of the valley's north wall, including Upper and Lower Yosemite Falls.

Hiking this stretch of Yosemite Valley's floor delivers a view lost to most motorists. When you get away from what John Muir termed "blunt-nosed mechanical beetles," and set out afoot, the scale and grandeur of all that stone meeting sky—Royal Arches, North Dome, Clouds Rest, Half Dome and more—increases exponentially.

Isn't it romantic?

Well, a lot of people think so. Yellow Pine Beach and Sentinel Beach along the Merced River are favorite sites for weddings. Cross Southside Drive to visit the fine facilities and check out the nuptials-friendly scene: a pretty part of the river, lovely meadows and views of Yosemite Falls.

Back on the trail, cross Sentinel Creek and after another 0.25 mile passes a junction with Four-Mile Trail that ascends to Glacier Point. Continue another 0.25 mile and cross Southside Drive to Swinging Bridge Picnic Area. Hike over the bridge and return to Yosemite Lodge via the paved bike path that skirts Leidig Meadow.

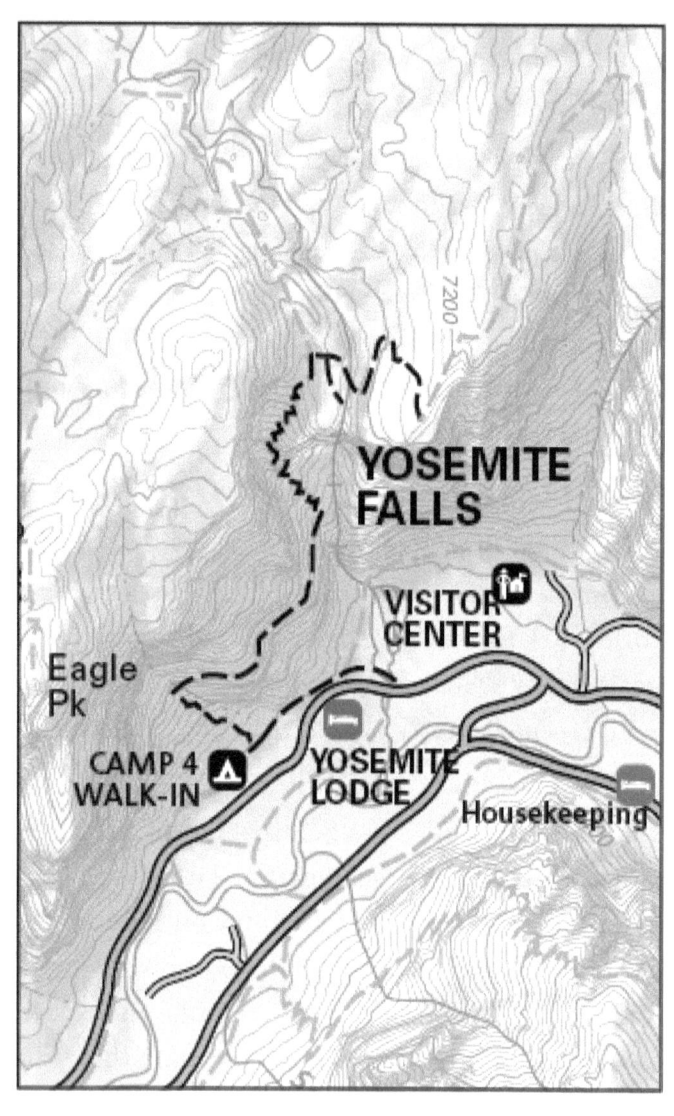

YOSEMITE FALLS

YOSEMITE FALLS TRAIL

From valley to Upper Yosemite Falls is 7.6 miles round trip with 2,500-foot elevation gain

Truly it's a wonder—a three-tiered cascade combining the 1,430-foot upper Yosemite Falls, the 675-foot middle falls and 320-foot lower Yosemite Falls. That adds up to a total height of 2,425 feet, earning Yosemite the honor of highest waterfall in North America.

Most Yosemite Valley visitors pay homage to Yosemite Falls, third-highest waterfall in the world, by walking 0.25 mile to the base of the lower falls. A much more difficult trail leads to the top of the upper falls. Looking up at Yosemite Falls from its base offers one perspective; watching it spill over the brink from the top is another memorable experience.

Until 2005, when a major decade-long renovation was completed on the $13.5 million "Yosemite Falls Project," the approach to Yosemite Falls was hardly scenic. Dozens of tour buses spewing diesel fumes idled in a football field-sized parking lot. As many as 10,000 people a day marched past a hideous cinderblock restroom and up a crumbling asphalt pathway to view the falls.

Now the environs at the foot of Yosemite Falls, a primary attraction for park visitors, look lots better: new paths, bridges over branches of Yosemite Creek and a restroom resembling a chalet. Interpretive markers explain the ecology, and there's a shrine to John Muir, who lived at the base of the falls in 1869 and 1870.

One of the park's oldest trails, the path climbs the airy heights to the precipice of Upper Yosemite Falls and rewards the hard-working hiker with magnificent views of Yosemite Valley. The trail's steepness scares off some hikers, but many more remain undaunted and make the strenuous (to say the least) climb.

Best time to visit is in spring when snowmelt swells the falls to their most spectacular. The upper part of the trail is dangerous in winter conditions.

DIRECTIONS: Begin at the Yosemite Falls trailhead, Camp 4, shuttle stop #7. Best parking is near Yosemite Lodge or the day-use lot south of Yosemite Village. If you can't find a convenient parking place, park at some distance away and take the free shuttle to the trailhead.

THE HIKE: Wasting no time, the path climbs steeply in the company of oaks, zigzagging upward via more than 40 tight switchbacks. A mile later, you'll near Columbia Rock, and 0.25 mile farther get a spectacular vista of Upper Yosemite Fall; this is a good turnaround point. Savor the view of Yosemite Valley located 1,000 feet below.

After another 0.5 mile, the path nears Lower Yosemite Falls; take the unmarked spur trail to the railing to view it. Soon after, it's more switchbacks and before long you leave behind the trees for a rockier world.

Proceed over shadeless terrain to the winter closure gate, and then a quarter mile more (making two right turns) to the overlook at the brink of the waterfall. The main path crosses the creek on a footbridge and ascends 0.75 mile to Yosemite Point and terrific views.

A steep ascent—with 40 switchbacks no less—on Yosemite Falls Trail leads to the highest waterfall in North America.

John Muir claimed Hetch Hetchy was second only to Yosemite Valley in its grandeur.

EVERY TRAIL TELLS A STORY.

III
Big Oak Flat Entrance

HIKE ON.

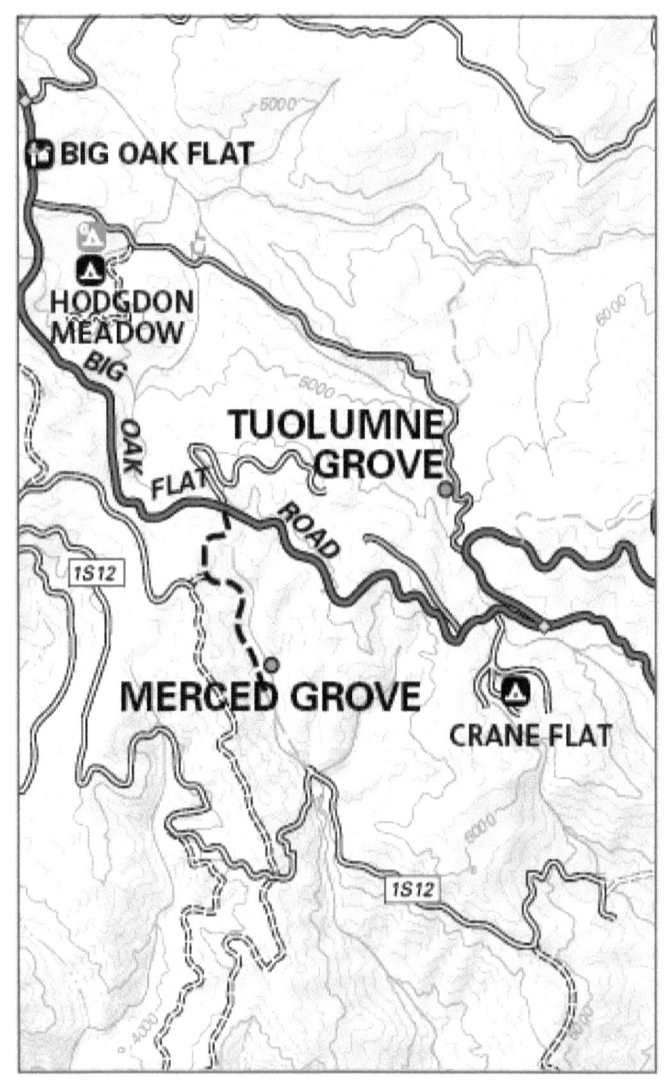

Tuolumne Grove

Tuolumne Grove Trail

From Tioga Road To Tuolumne Grove is 2.5 miles round trip with 500-foot elevation gain

Tuolumne Grove stands tall for hikers. Chief attraction is Dead Giant, a gargantuan sequoia stump tunneled in 1878 in order that horse-drawn wagons, and later automobiles, could drive through it.

DIRECTIONS: Tuolumne Grove is located off Tioga Road just 0.5 mile north of its intersection with Big Oak Flat Road.

THE HIKE: Descend through a mixed forest on the paved road. About a mile out, reach the first giant sequoias. A signed right fork leads to the Dead Giant. Walk on through and descend to a picnic area situated amidst more huge sequoias. From the picnic area, a 0.25-mile dirt trail loops through the tall trees.

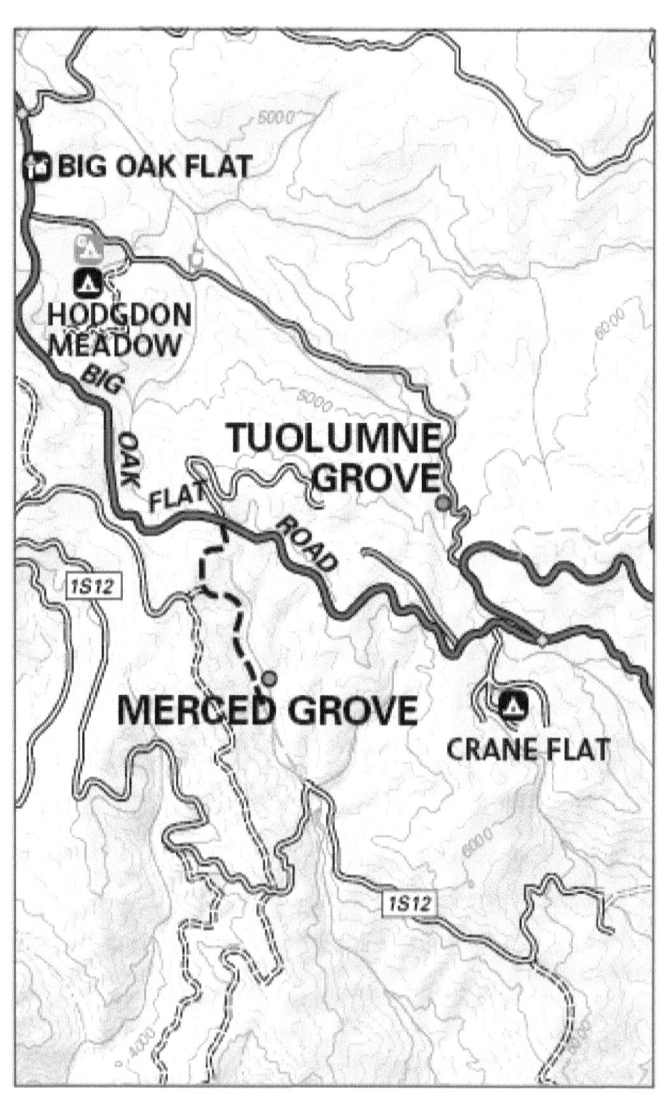

MERCED GROVE

MERCED GROVE TRAIL

To Merced Grove is 3 miles round trip with 400-foot elevation gain

Tucked into a remote western pocket of the park, Merced Grove is far less visited than Mariposa and Tuolumne, Yosemite's other sequoia groves. By tree count (20 or so), it's the smallest grove and requires the longest walk in order to reach it.

Thus the hiker looking for solitude among the sequoias might just find it in Merced Grove or, at least be assured that the trail will be shared with only a few kindred spirits.

The path to the grove is a dirt road, one of the first carriage roads created during the early horse-and-buggy days of the national park. In later years, grove visitors drove their autos down the road to Merced Grove.

Now the road is for hikers only. Park rangers haven't posted any interpretive signs or built any facilities in the grove, so the hiker comes away with the same feeling of wonder and discovery that the grove's first visitors might have had.

Actually, the National Park Service did build one structure in the grove long ago—a log cabin. The Russell Cabin or Merced Grove Cabin, as it's sometimes called, served as a ranger station and as an occasional retreat for the park superintendent. The cabin is in fine shape but it's boarded-up and not currently used.

DIRECTIONS: From the junction or Highway 120 Tioga Road and Big Oak Flat Road (also Highway 120) proceed west on the latter road 3.7 miles (that's 3.5 miles past Crane Flat Campground) to the signed turnout for Merced Grove on the left (south) side of the road. The signed trail departs from the small parking area.

THE HIKE: The fairly level road travels through a mixed forest. At first, tree-lovers are apt to cringe a bit when they look to the west of the road and see so many fire-destroyed trees.

However, the tree vistas soon improve. At the half-mile mark, you'll reach a signed junction, fork left, and begin a steep descent among an inspiring mixture of ponderosa pine, sugar pine, incense cedar and white fir.

Merced Grove

After a mile's descent from the junction, you'll reach the first sequoias—a half-dozen fine specimens located to the right of the road. A tiny creek trickles between two of the giants.

Walk a few more minutes down the road to the old ranger cabin and more inspiring tall trees. Sketchy trails lead down to the creek and more sequoias, but most hikers will be content to linger by the cabin then retrace their steps back to the trailhead.

Solitude among the sequoia. Merced is Yosemite's smallest and least visited grove.

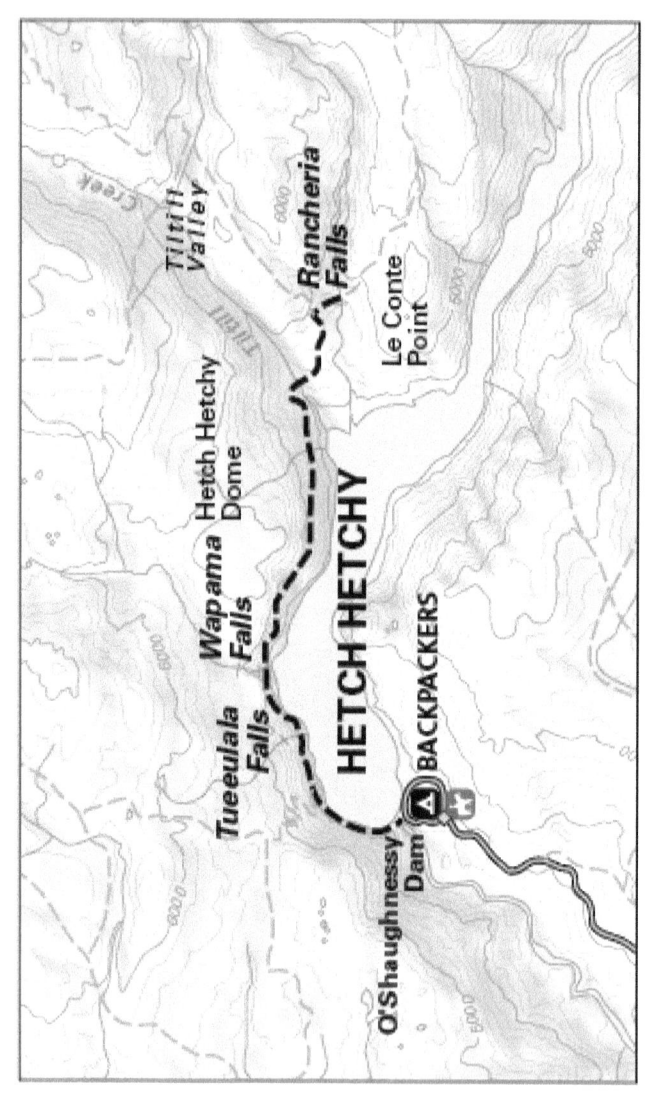

TheTrailmaster.com

HETCH HETCHY

HETCH HETCHY TRAIL

To Wapama Falls is 4 miles round trip; to Rancheria Falls is 13 miles round trip with 800-foot elevation gain

Perhaps no one living now remembers how Hetch Hetchy Valley looked before it was flooded. It certainly looks beautiful in the old photographs and paintings we can view today. Early 20th century travel books and descriptions by conservationists, including John Muir who struggled mightily to save Hetch Hetchy, say that it was second only to Yosemite Valley in grandeur.

When O'Shaughnessy Dam was completed in 1923 and the waters of the Tuolumne River impounded, the valley became an eight mile-long reservoir, providing water for the city of San Francisco, a function it still provides today.

We can imagine how the pre-dam valley appeared while hiking along its northern wall. Even with its floor flooded, the valley is something to behold.

Like Yosemite Valley, the Hetch Hetchy area is characterized by dramatic granite domes, cliffs and crags. Both valleys display the handiwork of ancient glaciers, and both boast mighty waterfalls.

Wapama Falls spills 1,200 feet over a granite precipice. At the end of the hike is tiny Rancheria Falls, providing a little water music for an inspiringly situated trail camp.

Linking the waterfalls is a path along the north side of Hetch Hetchy Reservoir. It's a fairly low elevation pathway, and therefore makes an enticing early-in-the-season Sierra jaunt. In spring, the waterfalls are at their most vigorous; however, bridges can be inundated at times of high water and should not be crossed in such conditions.

DIRECTIONS: From Highway 120, a mile west of Big Oak Flat entrance station, take the Hetch Hetchy turnoff and follow Evergreen Road, then Hetch Hetchy Road 16 miles to its end at the parking lot above O'Shaughnessy Dam and Hetch Hetchy Reservoir.

THE HIKE: Proceed across the dam and past some interpretive plaques. Look to the north side of the canyon to view Hetch Hetchy Dome and Wapama Falls.

Travel through a 500-foot long tunnel and emerge to join an old road that in turn leads over gray pine-dotted slopes.

A mile out, you'll reach a junction and head right (east) as the road gives way to a footpath. In another half-mile, pass by seasonal Tueeulala Falls and in another half mile spot Wapama Falls, soon reached by winding trail.

With the falls roaring in your ears, cross a couple branches of Fall Creek on a series of wood and steel bridges and carefully climb oak- and poison oak-covered slopes.

About 4 miles out, the trail levels, crosses a footbridge over a creek at 5 miles, and climbs past inviting swimming holes and water slides located along the creek. At the 6-mile mark, reach a junction with a connector trail that leads to a Ponderosa pine- and incense cedar-shaded campsite located below Rancheria Falls.

Stick with the main trail for another half-mile to reach a bridge over Rancheria Creek that's located just above the falls.

EVERY TRAIL TELLS A STORY.

IV

Tioga Pass

HIKE ON.

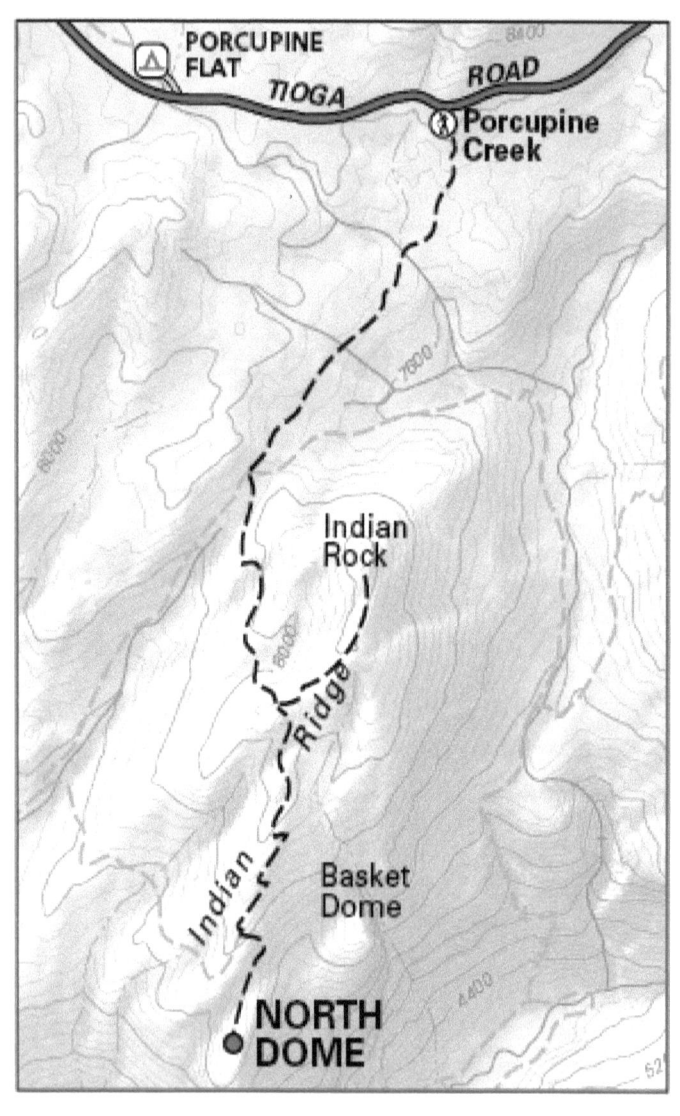

NORTH DOME

PORCUPINE CREEK, NORTH DOME TRAILS

From Tioga Road to Indian Ridge Arch is 6.1 miles round trip; to North Dome summit is 9 miles round trip with 600-foot elevation gain

Reaching the top of North Dome rewards hikers with a captivating and complete panorama of Yosemite Valley. Half Dome fans say the Yosemite icon offers superior views, but North Dome devotees point out that North Dome offers something Half Dome can't provide—a view of Half Dome! Plus a panorama of polished stone that includes Clouds Rest, Glacier Point and Sentinel Dome.

From a Yosemite Valley floor perspective, 7,542-foot North Dome dominates the north wall of Tenaya Canyon opposite Half Dome. It appears impossible to ascend but, surprisingly, the rounded mass of granite can be traveled and topped by a moderately graded pathway.

The path to the dome begins at Porcupine Flat, home to scores of the namesake creature, whose favorite food source is the inner bark of conifers and lodgepole pines in particular. A generous selection of other Yosemite trees may be glimpsed en route: Western white pine, Jeffrey pine, red fir and huckleberry oak. Several life zones overlap at this elevation (about 8,000 feet), creating this intriguing collection.

Extra added attraction for the hike is Indian Rock, an unusual stone arch perched atop Indian Ridge. The delicate, 20-foot arch, scarcely one-foot thick at its thickest part, is not Yosemite's only arch (another is below the surface of the Tuolumne River in Tuolumne Meadows), but it is the only one accessible to hikers.

DIRECTIONS: Signed North Dome trailhead is located off Tioga Road (Highway 120) some 24 miles east of Crane Flat and one mile east of Porcupine Flat Campground.

THE HIKE: Follow an old campground road (first paved, then dirt) for 0.7 mile. The route narrows to signed Porcupine Creek Trail, crosses two branches of Porcupine Creek, and wanders through the forest for another 0.8 mile.

At the 1.5-mile mark, intersect Snow Creek Trail. Walk right a dozen paces, veer left almost immediately at a second junction and begin a mellow ascent of Indian Ridge. Two miles out, the tree cover parts to permit a so-so view of Yosemite Valley. A switchbacking climb leads to a saddle and to a signed side trail to

Indian Rock. (Indian Rock Connector Trail, 0.25 mile long, ascends steeply up rocky Indian Ridge, gains the ridgetop, and travels it north to the arch.)

From the saddle, North Dome Trail descends along the forested crest of Indian Ridge for 1.2 miles to meet the trail to Yosemite Falls about 4 miles from the trailhead. Turn left and descend tight switchbacks to the shoulder of North Dome, then across the top of the long, bald dome.

Savor the incomparable view of the Merced River flowing through Yosemite Valley far below and identify the waterfalls cascading from the valley walls. Along with El Capitan, Three Brothers and the other prominent landmarks, observe Little Yosemite Valley and Mt. Starr King.

North Dome looks inaccessible, but a surprisingly mellow trail leads to the top and captivating panoramas of Yosemite Valley.

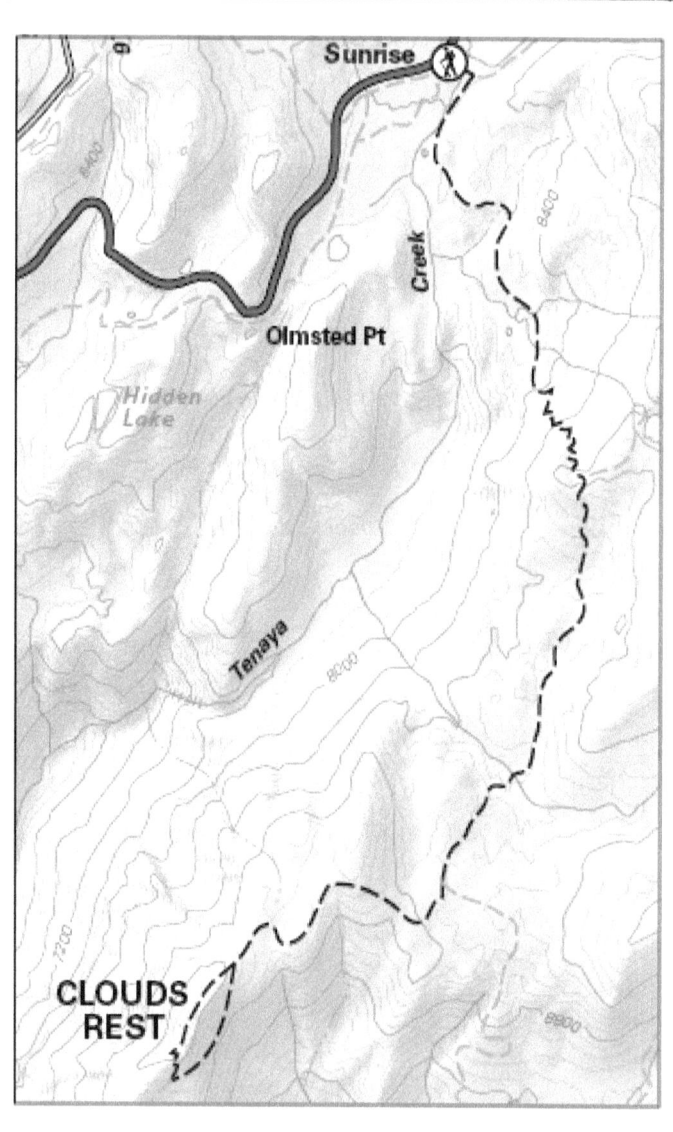

TheTrailmaster.com

Clouds Rest

Sunrise Lakes, Clouds Rest Trails

From Tenaya Lake to Sunrise Lakes is 10 miles round trip; to Clouds Rest is 14 miles round trip with 2,300-foot elevation gain

Climb to where the clouds rest, 9,926 feet high in the sky. Clouds Rest is higher than Half Dome, and is safer and easier to climb.

In addition, Clouds Rest offers better views than the famed Yosemite icon, some hikers say. From atop Clouds Rest, Yosemite's largest granite face, savor a panorama of rounded domes and sharp ridges, as well as the pageantry of Yosemite Valley.

You'll likely have company on the way to Clouds Rest but nowhere near the traffic encountered on the trail to Half Dome. While an easier hike than the one up Half Dome, the path to Clouds Rest is far from easy.

DIRECTIONS: From Highway 120 (Tioga Pass Road) 9 miles west of the Tuolumne Meadows Visitor Center, and some 16 miles east of White Wolf, proceed to the Sunrise Lakes Trailhead parking. You can also ride the Tuolumne Meadows shuttle bus to the stop by the parking area.

THE HIKE: Follow the signs for Sunrise High Sierra Camp, cross Tenaya Creek (no bridge: you might have to wade across in spring) and make your way across meadowland and among stands of lodgepole pine.

After 1.5 miles of minimal pain and gain, the ascent stiffens, gaining one thousand feet in the next 1.3 miles and reaching a junction. The trail to the three Sunrise Lakes and Sunrise Lakes High Sierra Camp, as well as to a junction with John Muir Trail, heads left (east).

Continue straight (south), dropping from the ridgetop to the base of Sunrise Mountain. Soon you climb again and reach another junction at the 5-mile mark. The left-branching trail leads to Sunrise Creek; the path also junctions the John Muir Trail.

Tramp through thinning forest toward a rocky ridge. At the seven-mile mark, reach a junction, signed even, but not the most obvious of intersections. If you miss this turnoff to the summit of Clouds Rest, fear not, for the lower trail, used by stock, continues to a point where you can doubleback and get up to the summit.

Any way you go, carefully climb the stacked layers of granite to the summit. Clouds Rest is not in the center of the park, but it is in the middle of all the sights Yosemite visitors come to see, including eye-popping views of Half Dome and more distant vistas all the way to Matterhorn Peak.

Looking at Clouds Rest is like taking Glacier Geology 101, whereby granite is uplifted from deep within the earth by massive tectonics, eroded by rains and rivers, and smoothed and polished by glaciers. We have glaciers to thank for sculpting the sheer faces in the granite that we so admire, particularly when water rushes over the top of them in the form of spectacular waterfalls. Clouds Rest is a truly epic expanse of granite, but be careful: there's a 5,000-foot drop-off from the top of its northwest face to Tenaya Canyon.

Clouds Rest: higher than Half Dome and safer and easier to climb.

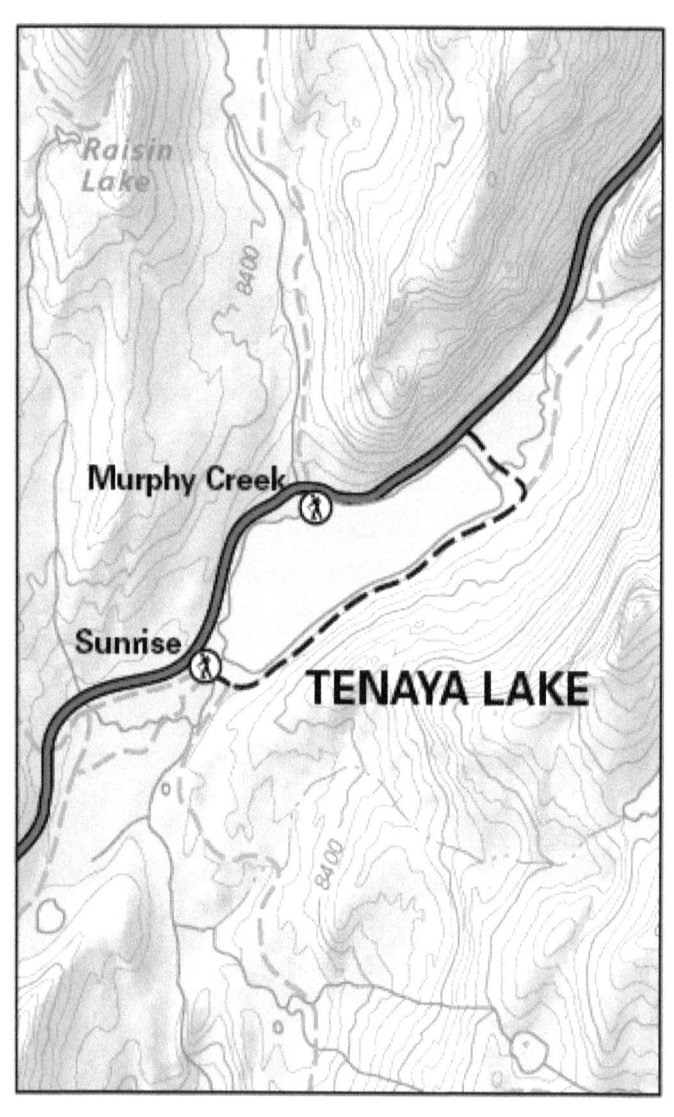

TENAYA LAKE

TENAYA LAKE TRAIL

2.4 miles round trip

Tenaya makes everybody's Top Ten High Sierra Lakes list. While you can see Tenaya from the highway, and can survey the lake from Olmsted Point, you'll appreciate it even more while walking Tenaya Lake Trail.

DIRECTIONS: From its junction with Big Oak Flat Road, follow Highway 120 (Tioga Road) 32 miles to the east end of Tenaya Lake and park in the picnic area.

THE HIKE: Walk along the sandy beach, then join the path along the lake's southeast shore, contouring through pine forest. The path continues to Olmsted Point. Or continue on the trail past its junction with the trail leading to Sunrise Lakes and back up to the parking area by Tioga Road.

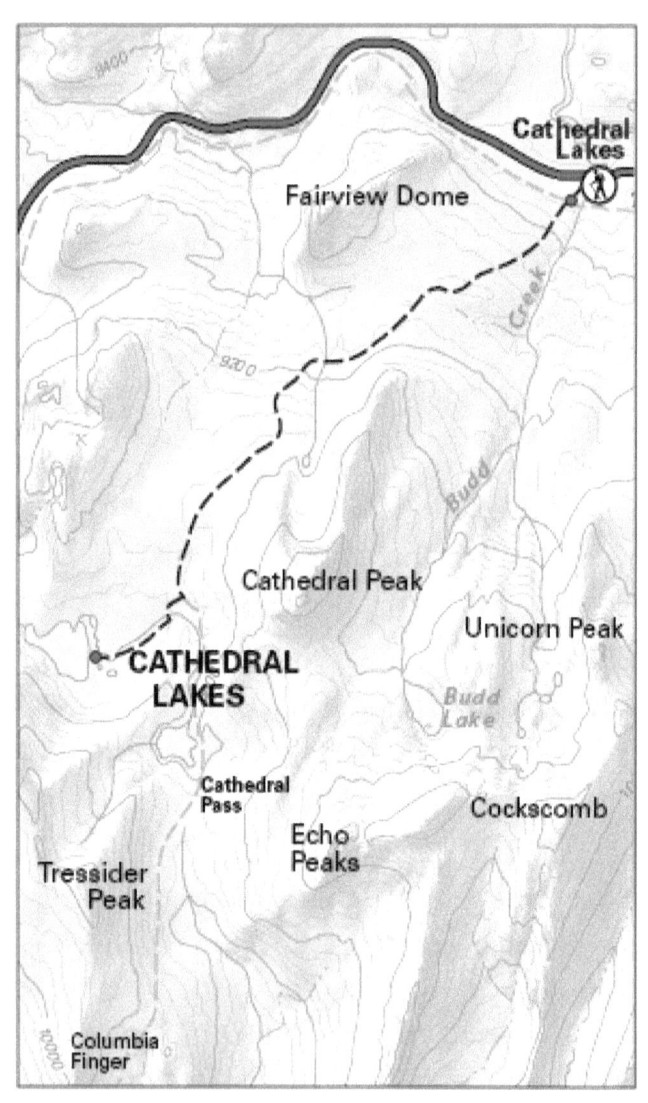

TheTrailmaster.com

CATHEDRAL LAKES
JOHN MUIR TRAIL

To Lower Cathedral Lake is 7.5 miles round trip with 1,000-foot elevation gain

Many of John Muir's effusive descriptions of the High Sierra have a spiritual tone, and refer to landscapes as sanctuaries, temples and cathedrals. "This I must say is the first time I've been to church in California," wrote John Muir after visiting the Cathedral Lakes and making the first recorded ascent of Cathedral Peak in 1869.

This hike offers a sampling of the John Muir Trail, with the great naturalist at our heels whispering: "Going to the mountains is going home."

DIRECTIONS: Parking is located on both shoulders of Highway 120 (Tioga Pass Road) 1.5 miles west of Tuolumne Campground entrance or some 24 miles east of White Wolf. In summer, ride the free shuttle bus to the trailhead by leaving your car at the Tuolumne Meadows Wilderness Permit station or Tenaya Lake.

THE HIKE: Walk 0.1 mile through the forest to a four-way junction. Proceed straight on steep John Muir Trail, which can be dusty and is steep going for the first 0.7 mile. The trail mellows for a time, passes among lodgepole pine and climbs again.

About a mile out, Cathedral Peak pops into view. Traverse meadowland made soggy by Cathedral Creek and assorted creeklets in the late spring and early summer, curve from southwest to south, and pass above a gurgling spring.

Two-plus miles of ascent gains a forested saddle. And then the path descends, Cathedral Peak appears on the skyline to your left, and three miles out, the trail divides. (JMT leads another half mile to upper Cathedral Lake and its shoreline campsites, handsomely backdropped by craggy Cathedral Peak (10,911 feet) in the east and ten thousand footers Echo and Tressider Peaks rising above the south shore. Hike a few more minutes up the Muir Trail to Cathedral Pass and get a grand view of Cathedral Lakes Basin.)

Head west (right) to Cathedral Lake. The path descends through the woods and crosses a branch of Cathedral Creek. Turn right and follow the watercourse down-creek. Try to stay on the main trail (as opposed to one of the use trails) as you cross the meadow. The meadow is known to be muddy and you might have to hike through it in over-your-boot-deep water and/or mud to reach Cathedral Lake, a popular weekend backpacker destination.

Around the lake, geologic history is written in the rocks. Lakeside granite slabs offer flat spots for sunning and picnicking. Near the lake are curious erratics: ice-transported boulders that were left here when the glaciers melted. Make your way to the far end of the lake and gaze westward for a bird's eye view of Tenaya Lake, located just a mile away.

For those hikers looking for a longer return route, I heartily recommend returning to the JMT, ascending to Sunrise Camp and looping over and down to Tenaya Lake on Tioga Road. (Total distance is 13 miles for the day) In summer, the park's shuttle bus service links the Cathedral Lakes Trailhead and Tenaya Lake.

From Cathedral Lakes, get a great view of Cathedral Peak and Eichorn Pinnacle.

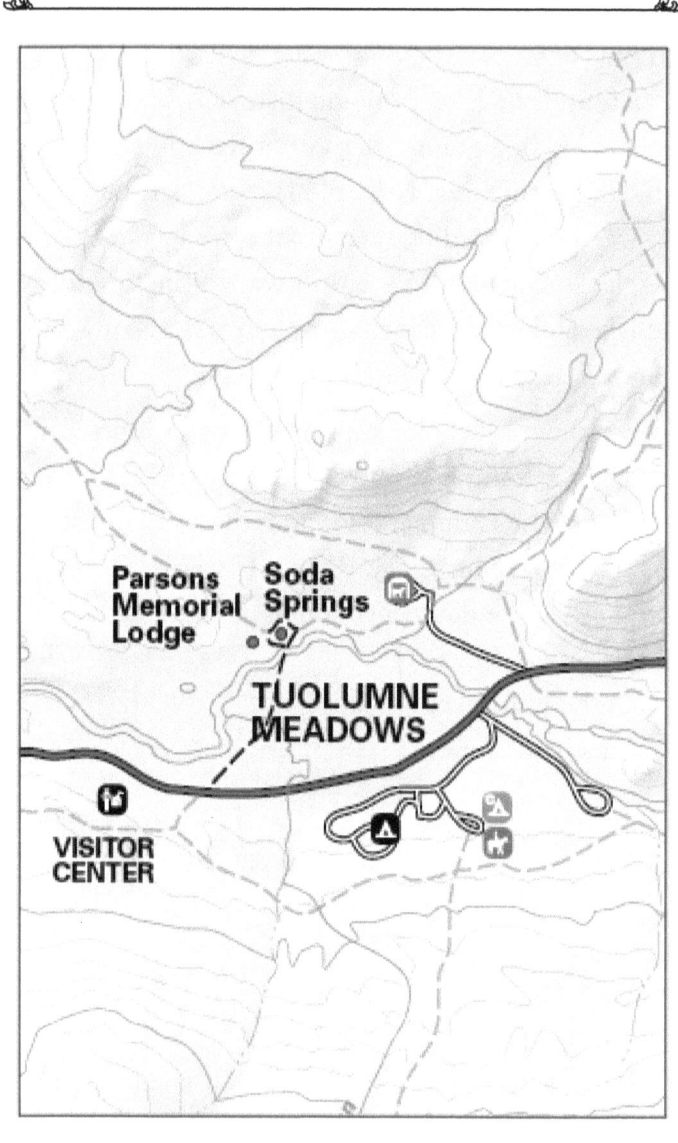

Tuolumne Meadows

Tuolumne Meadows Trail

From Tioga Road to Parsons Lodge and Soda Springs is 1.5 miles round trip

Lush and lovely Tuolumne Meadow is likely the national park's best known site outside of Yosemite Valley and for good reason. Easily accessible by short trails, the High Sierra's largest sub-alpine meadow is a glorious, wildflower-splashed basin ringed by forested slopes, roundish domes and sharp summits.

John Muir's first summer in the Sierra was spent as a shepherd, tending a flock of some 2,000 sheep pastured in Tuolumne Meadows. Muir's journals of that time are filled with the wonders of nature he observed along with his first thoughts about the preservation of Yosemite. Muir soon realized that sheep, which he later characterized as "hoofed locusts," and other grazing animals could destroy an alpine meadow.

Today a length of the John Muir Trail crosses the great naturalist's beloved Tuolumne Meadows. Other paths lead to Parsons Memorial Lodge named for Edward Parsons, who fought alongside John Muir to preserve the park, Hetch Hetchy Valley and other wildlands during the early days of the Sierra Club. After Parsons, an accomplished photographer, outings leader and early Sierra Club President died in 1915, the Club constructed this lodge in his honor.

Parsons Lodge, long ago deeded to the National Park Service, has served as a reading room/library for generations of visitors. Many a hiker has found a cool retreat on a hot summer's day or taken refuge from an afternoon thunderstorm.

Interpretive signs posted sporadically along Tuolumne Meadows paths offer insights about Parsons, Muir, the old Tioga Road and the Native American tribes who visited the meadows for so many centuries. For more information about the meadows, visit Tuolumne Meadows Visitor Center (open summer only), located about 0.1 mile west of the trailhead on Tioga Road.

DIRECTIONS: I like to begin this ramble from the north side of Tioga Road, just 0.1 mile east of Tuolumne Meadows Visitor Center. Parking is along both sides of Tioga Road. Some hikers prefer to access the Tuolumne Meadows trail system from the Lembert Dome/Glen Aulin/Soda Springs trailhead located a little farther to the east.

Tuolumne Meadows

THE HIKE: The wide path extends north across the meadows. Families linger along the bends of the Tuolumne River to fish or to enjoy one of the best picnic spots on the planet.

Cross the wooden bridge over the Tuolumne River, bend left along the river and take the signed trail forking right to Parsons Memorial Lodge. From the lodge, follow the signed path very briefly east to Soda Springs, a muddy area where carbonated water percolates up from the ground.

The trail loops past some interpretive plaques then angles back toward the bridge over the Tuolumne River. From here, retrace your steps back to the trailhead.

The famed John Muir Trail meanders across Tuolumne Meadows.

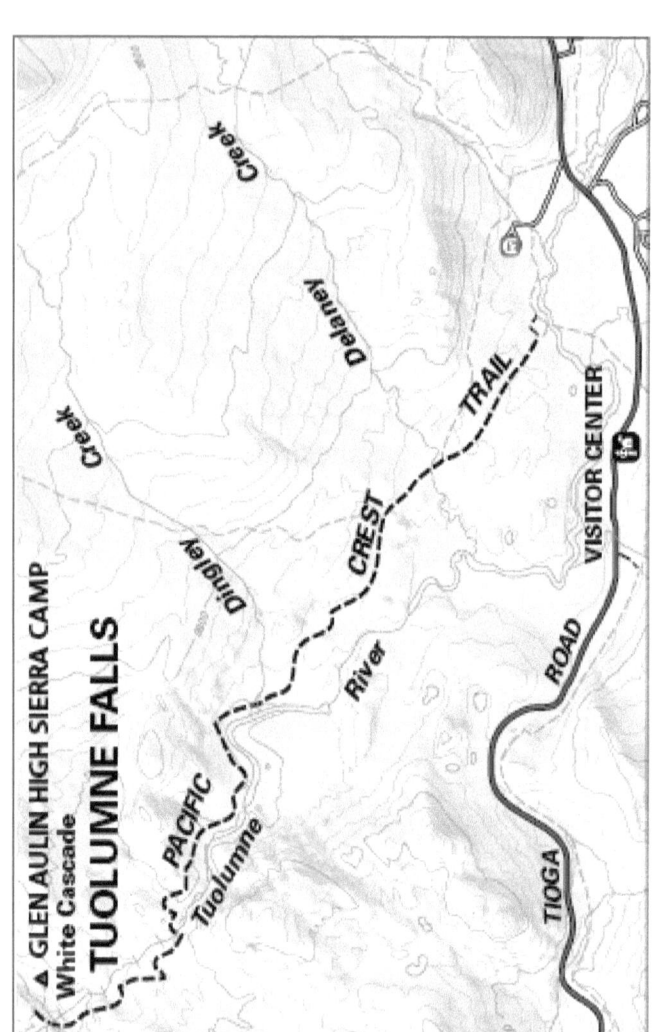

Tuolumne Falls
Pacific Crest Trail

To Tuolumne Falls is 9 miles round trip with 400-foot elevation gain

In a national park that boasts some of the world's best waterfalls, a relatively modest cascade such as Tuolumne Falls is apt to be overlooked. Not only is Tuolumne a fraction of the size of the park's famed falls, it's located far from Waterfall Central, the Yosemite Valley.

Tuolumne Falls' allure arises as much from the footpath that reaches it as the falls itself. It's a classic Yosemite backcountry hike along a sterling stretch of the Pacific Crest Trail, a glorious passage along the Tuolumne River, which mesmerizes with its glistening stones, shimmering pools and dancing rapids.

In one way, though, this is an atypical Yosemite high country hike; the trail doesn't climb a peak or pass, but instead descends quite modestly to a waterfall.

DIRECTIONS: From Tioga Road, at the east end of Tuolumne Meadows, take the turnoff for Lembert Dome. Park at the base of the dome or, better yet, drive 0.3 mile down the dirt road to a locked gate and the signed trail for Glen Aulin. Park alongside the road near the gate.

THE HIKE: Tramp Old Tioga Road, a wagon road of 1883 vintage, as it edges along Tuolumne Meadows. Fork right after 0.4 mile and join the trail toward Soda Springs and Parsons Memorial Lodge. John Muir Trail heads south over the Tuolumne River bridge, while your route visits Soda Springs, where rust-tinted carbonated water bubbles up.

From the springs, follow signs to Glen Aulin and begin a mellow meander northwest that passes a junction with a trail from the stable after 0.8 mile, soon thereafter crosses a branch of Delaney Creek, and passes a junction with the trail to Young Lakes after another 0.4 mile of travel.

Traverse among great granite slabs and lodgepole pine. Where the trees give way, vistas open up to include Unicorn and Cathedral peaks.

Cross Dingley Creek to reach the Tuolumne River about 2.5 miles from the trailhead. PCT offers a 0.75-mile level contour along the river, then works its way up a granite outcropping that presents views of the river gorge below and Little Devil's Postpile on the opposite bank. This basalt pillar was named for its volcanic kinship to rock formations in Devil's Postpile National Monument.

Descend via rock stairs, cross the Tuolumne River on a bridge and head down-river alongside frisky cascades to reach the top of Tuolumne Falls. Continue descending with the trail to the base of the falls and past a lower Tuolumne Falls tumbler called White Cascade.

Want more waterfalls? PCT bends north, crosses another bridge over the Tuolumne and meets a short side path leading to Glen Aulin High Sierra Camp. Part company with northbound PCT and continue along the Tuolumne River to California Falls (13 miles round trip), LeConte Falls (15 miles round trip) and Waterwheel Falls (16 miles round trip with 2,000-foot elevation gain) to return to the trailhead.

Hikers love the footpath to Tuolumne Falls. A classic High Sierra day hike.

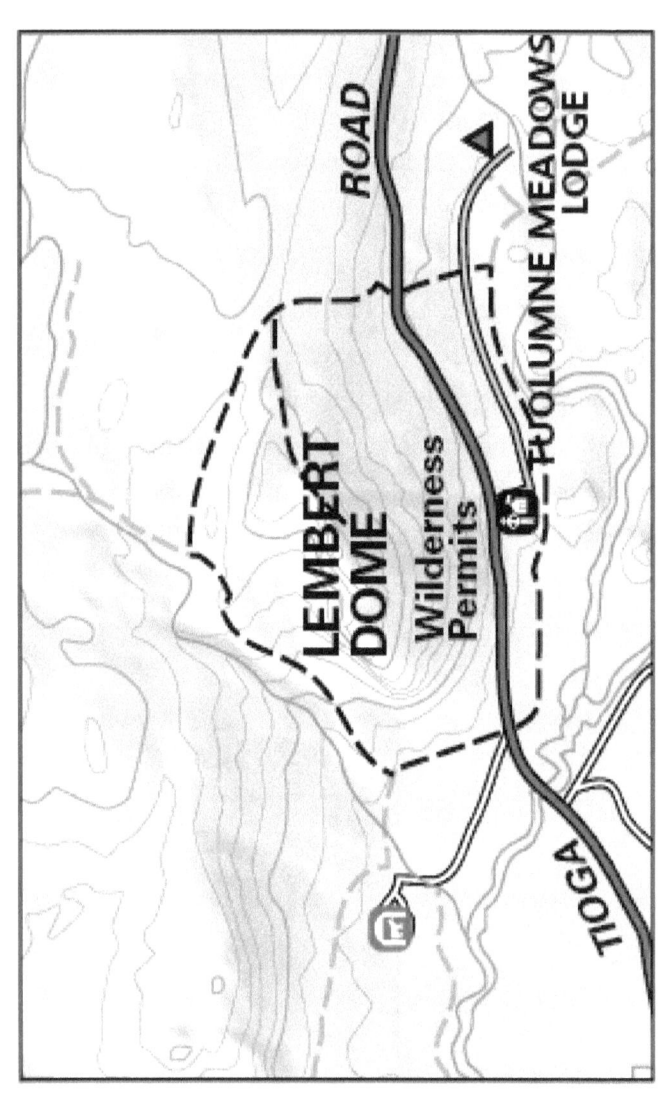

Lembert Dome

Lembert Dome Trail

To Lembert Dome is 3.25 miles round trip with 900-foot elevation gain

The 9,450-foot dome looks absolutely impossible to scale when regarding it from the trailhead, but fear not. For the time-short (but not stamina-short) traveler, able to do only one hike in the Tuolumne Meadows area, Lembert Dome is the one to do.

From atop the dome you'll have Tuolumne Meadows and Yosemite Valley at your feet, and view a parade of peaks from Cathedral Peak all the way to Mt. Dana at Tioga Pass.

Geologists say Lembert Dome is not a true dome (such as Sentinel Dome) but a *roche moutoonee*; the French phrase "rock sheep" describes a glacier-carved formation recognized by its sheer front and sloping back. The *roche moutonee* was named for shepherd/naturalist Jean Baptiste Lembert, who began work in Tuolumne Meadows in 1885. An unsolved mystery to this day is who shot him dead in his cabin—and why—in 1896.

DIRECTIONS: From Tioga Road (Highway 120) at the east end of Tuolumne Meadows, located the Lembert Dome parking area on the north side of the road.

THE HIKE: Leave behind the picnic area and restrooms and head north from the Dog Lake/Lembert Dome trailhead sign. Traverse a rock slab to a fork in the trail at 0.1 mile. Continue north to a junction and toward Dog Lake, ignoring two more trails from the stables coming in from the left (west) and staying right (north) on the main path and ascending through lodgepole pine forest.

Just over a mile out, the path forks. (The left fork ascends north to Dog Lake, one of Yosemite's warmest lakes.)

The path to Lembert Dome passes a little pond perched in the shadow of the dome. At the 1.75-mile mark, intersect the signed 0.3-mile (with 350 feet of elevation gain) summit trail to the dome.

The path picks its way westward over a ridgeline, tree-spiked at lower elevation, treeless at higher elevation, gaining the granite-slabbed shoulder of the dome. When the trail gives out, choose a route over the bare rock and zigzag your way to the top.

Lembert Dome

Enjoy grand vistas over Lyell Canyon and the Cathedral Range and admire the park's highest peaks including Mt. Florence (12,561 feet) and Mt. Lyell (13,114 feet).

Backtrack on the summit path to the main trail. Head right (south) and switchback steeply downhill 0.75 mile to Tioga Road. Carefully cross the road and hike 0.1 mile to a parking lot and the access road extending to Tuolumne Meadows Lodge. Cross this little road and, still heading south, notice a sign for John Muir Trail. Head west on a path that parallels the road from Tuolumne Lodge to Wilderness Center and also parallels Tioga Road for about 0.75 mile until it reaches a point opposite the parking area for Lembert Dome. Cross Tioga Road to return to the trailhead.

Choose a route over the bare rock and zigzag your way to the top of Lembert Dome.

Mt Dana
Meadows
Mono Pass Trailhead
Dana Fork
Dana
Parker Pass Creek
Mt Gibbs
Mammoth Peak
Kuna Lake
MONO PASS
Summit Lake
Kuna Crest
Bingaman Lake
Spillway Lake
Parker Pass
Parker Pass Lake
Helen Lake

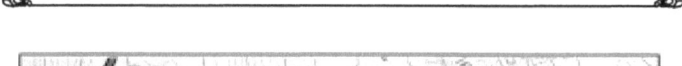

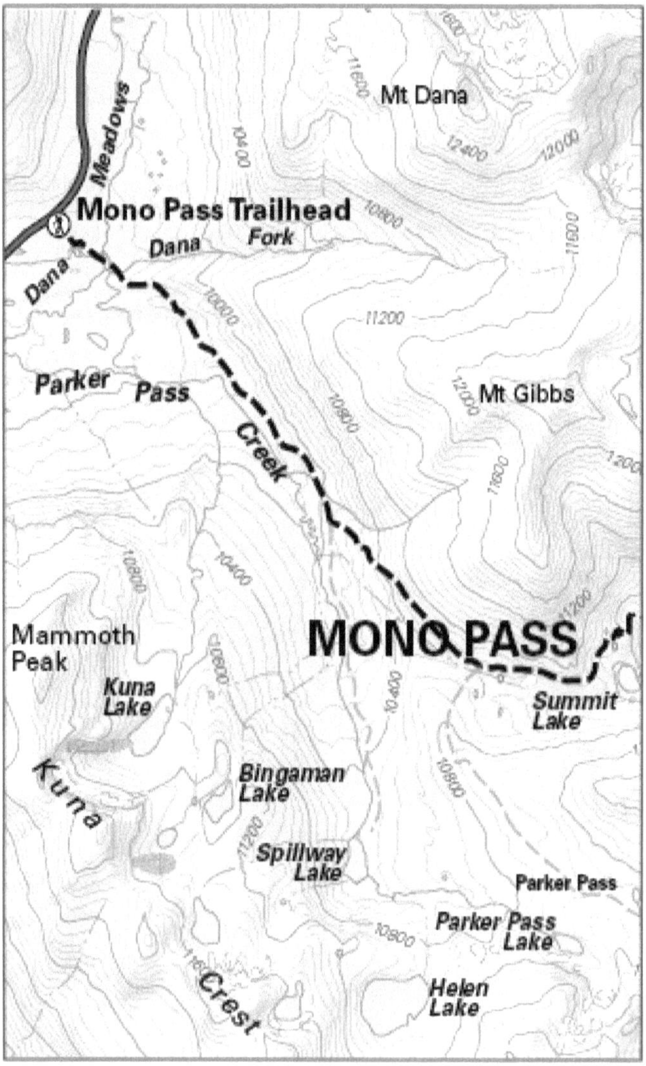

Mono Pass

Mono Trail

From Dana Meadows to Mono Pass is 8 miles round trip with a 900-foot elevation gain

A historic trail leading to a historic pass, as well as stirring views from the eastern Sierra crest, are some of the highlights of a hike to Mono Pass.

Mono Pass is located on Yosemite's eastern boundary where the national park meets Inyo National Forest and the Ansel Adams Wilderness. From the often wind-whipped pass, the view encompass Mono Lake and surrounding arid lands, as well as the White Mountains on the California-Nevada border.

This hike—a modest effort by Sierra standards—yields big rewards: alpine lakes, mountains, meadows and panoramic views; for these reasons, Mono is fairly popular trail.

Long before Yosemite became a national park, Native Americans traveled Mono Trail, which extended from the slopes above the west end of

Yosemite Valley up to Porcupine Flat and then along a route much like that of today's Tioga Road. Mono Trail then surmounted Mono Pass and descended infamous Bloody Canyon, so-named by early prospectors and explorers for the sharp rocks that bloodied—and often killed—their horses and mules.

En route, you'll pass several prospectors' cabins, habitation for miners working the Golden Crown Mine in the 1880s. Some of the dwellings, constructed of material at hand—local whitebark pine—are in better shape than you might imagine considering the long and severe winters that occur here at two miles high in elevation.

DIRECTIONS: Mono Pass Trailhead is located at a pullout off Tioga Road (Highway 120), 1.5 miles west of the national park's Tioga Pass entry station. The trailhead is at Dana Meadows on the south side of the road.

THE HIKE: You'll begin in the company of lodgepole pine, but soon leave them behind as the trail crosses Dana Meadows. At 0.5 mile, boulder-hop across the Tuolumne River and start a moderate ascent over a glacial moraine.

A bit more than a mile out, you'll pass a collapsing log cabin, and soon enter a sweet-smelling land of pine and sage, populated by legions of ground squirrels.

About 2.2 miles out, Mono Trail junctions Spillway Lake Trail (a 2-mile pathway that leads to a little lake.)

Now Mono Trail begins climbing in earnest, passing the remains of another miner's cabin at the 3-mile mark and climbing to a junction with the spur trail leading (0.25 miles) to several more silver miners' cabins.

Continue to the top of 10,604-foot Mono Pass, which marks the boundary of Yosemite National Park. For the best views, press on a short 0.5 mile into Inyo National Forest to a point overlooking the head of Bloody Canyon. Savor views of Mono Lake and dry terrain, both flat and mountainous, to the east.

A historic trail leads to historic Mono Pass.

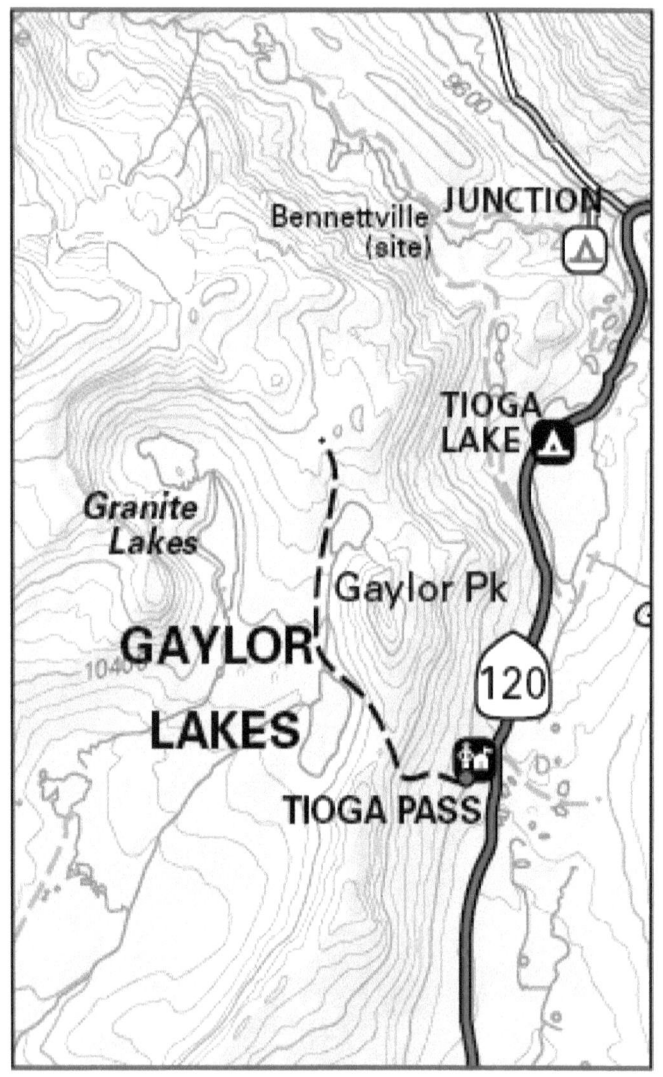

Gaylor Lakes

Gaylor Lakes Trail

From Tioga Pass to Gaylor Lakes is 4 miles round trip with 900-foot elevation gain

On the hike to Gaylor Lakes you're guaranteed to feel the high in the High Sierra. The climb begins in the shadow of Tioga Pass Entrance Station at nearly 10,000 feet in elevation. It's the highest trailhead in the park.

The path climbs through the rarefied air to Gaylor Lakes, two cobalt gems rimmed by dramatic crags. Marvel at hillsides known to bloom with lupine, columbine and corn lily. Daisy, Sierra wallflower, penstemon and spreading phlox add to the trailside bouquet.

This hike also offers a walk into history. Near trail's end is the site of the Great Sierra Mine, *raison d'être* for the predecessor of Tioga Road, and an ambitious undertaking even by the standards of gold fever-crazed 19th century prospectors.

In 1881 the Great Sierra Mining Company hauled tons of machinery to Gaylor Lakes Basin and beyond and proceeded to drill and blast a 1,784-foot long main tunnel into the mountains back of upper Gaylor Lake.

For a few years the boomtown of Dana, complete with its own post office, thrived. Just north of Dana stood an even more remote town—Bennettville—headquarters of the mining company. After four futile years of digging, the miners abandoned efforts to uncover the rich vein of silver believed to lie buried here.

Beyond upper Gaylor Lake, hikers will discover an old stone cabin, a well-built structure with two foot-thick rock walls that dates from the 1880s. Other mine ruins are located near the cabin.

With so much scenery packed into a short hike, this trail is fairly popular (at least for a park pathway so far removed from Yosemite Valley). Get an early start to avoid the crowds.

DIRECTIONS: Head for Yosemite National Park's eastside entry station on Tioga Pass Road. Share trailhead parking with hikers bound for Mt. Dana in a lot west of the station.

THE HIKE: Begin with a very steep westward ascent, switchbacking over slopes seasonally sprinkled with wildflowers. Enjoy in-your-face views of Mt. Dana to the east.

Ascend past scattered whitebark pine and lodgepole pine. After a 0.75-mile ascent that seems much longer, crest a rocky ridge and behold Gaylor Lakes, commanding Gaylor Peak to the east and a collection of Cathedral Peaks to the west.

The path descends rapidly, losing hard-won elevation, to the first (Middle) Gaylor Lake, located one mile from the trailhead. From the lake, the path follows the inlet creek on a mellow eastern ascent. A mile of walking through meadows brings you to Upper Gaylor Lake, situated at about 10,500 feet in elevation.

Admire the lake's stirring backdrop of cone-shaped Gaylor Peak. Follow the trail around the left (north) side of the lake. A steep 0.1-mile ascent leads to the old stone cabin and the site of the Great Sierra Mine. A bit farther up the trail lie several mine shafts. (Keep away.)

From the highest trailhead in the park, hike through thin air to Gaylor Lakes, two gems rimmed by dramatic crags.

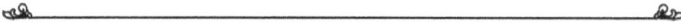

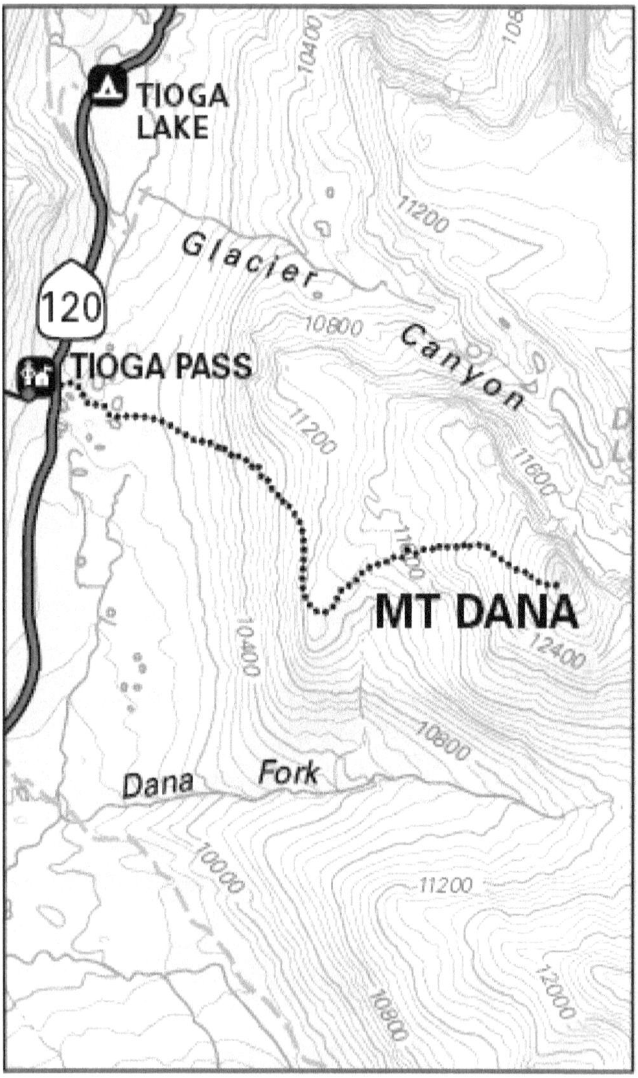
TIOGA
LAKE
Glacier
Canyon
120
TIOGA PASS
11200
10800
10400
11600
MT DANA
12400
Dana
Fork
10000
12000

Mt. Dana

From Tioga Pass to Mt. Dana summit is 6 miles round trip with 3,100-foot elevation gain

Mt. Dana, 13,057 feet high in the sky, is Yosemite's second-highest peak, and a climb to remember. Only Mt. Lyell is higher (by 57 feet), though it requires mountaineering skills to gain its summit.

The path ascending Mt. Dana is not a regularly maintained route, but a use trail, one established a long time ago. The route is the essentially the same one taken by Whitney Survey Party members William Brewer and Charles Hoffman, who first climbed the peak in 1863. Yosemite botanist extrordinaire, Dr. Carl Sharsmith, who worked more than a half-century in the park, helped design the modern route to reduce impact on the mountain's considerable alpine flora.

Dana Meadows and the boggy areas around two ponds offer abundant wildflower displays, as do the higher, drier slopes. The seasonal sprinkling includes

Indian paintbrush, alpine goldenrod, Columbine, spreading phlox and lots of lupine. Those clusters of blue you'll spot above 12,000 feet in elevation are sky pilot, which bloom in July and August.

At 9,941 feet, Tioga Pass gives the hiker quite a headstart toward the summit. Ordinarily, to reach such a high High Sierra summit, a much longer approach with a greater elevation gain is required. Because of the peak's relatively short approach, Dana has been a favorite peak to climb for generations of hikers.

You'll need a map—and perhaps a scorecard—to identify and record all the peaks you'll see from atop Mt. Dana. From the peaks on the park's western boundary—Mt. Lyell, Mt. Gibbs, and more—to peaks in the heart of Yosemite—Mt. Hoffman, Tuolumne Peak—this is a panorama to remember. The view also encompasses Saddlebag and Ellery lakes, just outside the park and Mono Lake and the Mojave Desert far to the east.

DIRECTIONS: Drive to Yosemite National Park's east entrance station on Highway 120 (Tioga Pass Road), some 12 miles east of Highway 395. Park in the lot south of the entrance station on the west side of the road. The trail begins on the east side.

THE HIKE: Begin with a moderate ascent through Dana Meadows, often wildflower-strewn in summer and a short cruise through lodgepole pine forest. After 0.5 mile, the real work begins. The going gets steeper and rockier with switchback after switchback. Trail markers help you stay on the right route.

Past timberline, you climb to a large rock cairn, about two miles from the trailhead and 11,500 feet in elevation. Here at the towering cairn, you get a good view of Mt. Dana's summit and say goodbye to the trail.

Choose from a variety of use paths. A cairn-marked trail/route helps the hiker to ascend that last long mile (gaining 1,400 feet) to the summit.

A magnificent panorama of peaks is the hiker's reward for the steep ascent of Mt. Dana, Yosemite's second-highest peak.

Yosemite Stories

The Yo-Semite Falls
Lithograph by Thomas A. Ayres (1855).

EVERY TRAIL TELLS A STORY.

"A Trip to the Yohamite Valley"
by Thomas A. Ayres
Published in the San Francisco Daily Alta California, August 6, 1859. Ayres, a San Francisco artist, drew the first sketches of Yosemite Falls

Glad to escape the intense excitement which still unfortunately prevails in our city, I left by the Stockton steamer, June 16th, on a second trip to the celebrated Valley of the Yohemity and the sources of the Merced River.

Mounting our animals, we soon reached "Crane Flat," a large meadow surrounded by the lofty forest, and adorned with brilliant flowers. Here the trail leads to the right, leaving the divide to the left, and descending into the waters of Cascade Creek and its tributaries. Ascending and descending several steep spurs and crossing several streams, we finally caught a glimpse of the everlasting walls of the Yohemity, and farther on we saw gleaming like a silver thread from the dark precipice, the "Cascade of the Rainbow [Bridalveil Falls]."

We now commenced the descent into the valley in earnest, and in an hour reached the level of the river, by a good though very steep trail, constructed by the enterprising citizens of Coulterville. Nature has done more for the descent by the Mariposa trail, but the route from Coulterville reaches the valley at a lower altitude (an important consideration, on account of the snows early in the season, when the falls are to be seen in their glory); it also avoids the dangerous crossing of the South Fork [Illilouette Creek] on the Mariposa side. Yet the first view of the valley as seen from the Mariposa road is the best, and produces an impression never to be forgotten.

Resuming our journey up the valley, the first object that attracts our attention is the Cascade of the Rainbow, descending into the valley on our right from a height of nine hundred and twenty eight feet. The water comes over the sharp granite edge of the precipice, then descending, is broken into fleecy forms, sometimes swayed hither and thither by the wayward winds; at other times the sun lights up its spray with all the colors of the rainbow, hanging like a prismatic veil from the somber cliff. The surrounding peaks are riven into varied forms, most picturesque in their outlines, contrasting beautifully with the emerald meadows and masses of pines, cedars and oaks at their base. The stream has a large body of water, and has its source far away to the south, towards the divide of the San Joaquin River.

As we proceeded onward we were held in silent awe by the sublime proportions of "El Capitan," or the Chieftain of the Yohemity—a cliff of granite lifting its awful forms on the left to the height of three thousand one hundred feet—a sheer precipice jutting into the valley.

Traveling the Trails
from *Yosemite Tales and Trails* (1934) by Katharine Ames Taylor

That is the magic of maps. Cause and effect become blurred, and it is only a step from following a dotted black line across white paper, looking like a fever or population chart, to jogging along a mountain trail, skirting the skyline of the Sierras, or sauntering down by some still, forgotten lake.

Hikers, like all Gaul, they divide into three parts. There are the mountain climbers, who come either in bevies and clubs, or as free-lances, and adopt some mountain temporarily and cannot rest until they have scaled its peak, before going on to conquer new heights. There are the nature-lovers who don't care a hang what is on top of the mountain, who are lured by a trail not because it leads to the earth's high spots, but because it winds through woods and meadows and dells, across carpets of blossoms where wild flowers and wild animals can be stalked and studied at leisure. And there is the plain and lowly hiker, with his camera in his hand and perspiration on his brow, who outnumbers all the aforementioned gentry of the trail something like four to one. They are the ordinary folk, sick of the sight of old brick walls, longing for a look at the wilderness, hoofing it along a narrow path for no other reason than the sheer fun of it.

In spite of the six hundred miles of trail, which crisscross the Park, consider the thousands of acres of grandeur which have not yet been scratched. So that great and growing company of trail-trekkers will be safe for many years to come. Uncle Sam is attending to that. For he has limited the number of roads which can be built into any National Park, while increasing the trail projects. The balance of beauty still lies with the hiker, and he has only to shoulder his pack and swing up the trail to lose himself in an hour in as profound a solitude as the Lord ever created in his six days of world-making.

Up there in the Sierras, time is the coin of the realm. You are rich or poor, not according to the dollars, but to the days and the nights you have to spend. So hoard your hours like a miser, till you arrive, then spend them like a mountain millionaire, paying out a day to stroll across the roof of the world, an hour to lie beneath a tree which has taken three thousand years in the growing! Budget your time, so that none of it is squandered, then spend like a prodigal, and your interest will be compounded every year for the rest of your life.

Then there are the trails! The long ones and the short ones. The steep ones, and the steeper ones. The most traveled from the floor of the Valley are those to Vernal and Nevada Falls, the Four-Mile trail to Glacier, and the Ledge trail. Fewer seem to know about the Sierra Point trail, which is a fairly steep scramble, but a most rewarding one. It branches off from the Vernal Falls trail just above Happy Isles and spirals upward for three-quarters of a mile to a rocky promontory opposite Illilouette Falls, with Vernal and Nevada tumbling to the left of you, Yosemite plunging to the right. You are suspended, as it were, between heaven and earth, looking down upon the Valley, looking up to the Sierra peaks.

You cannot sit and watch Yosemite Falls booming over the cliffs without feeling the urge to climb to the top and peer behind the scenes. There is no way of describing the sensation you have as you stand beside that deafening roar of falling water where it slips over the brink of the precipice.

Half Dome is a challenge to both seasoned and tenderfoot hikers alike. Its very bulk and its polished dome seem to defy them. On the top of its rounded dome there are about eight acres of flat surface. A few scrubby tree bushes have found root-hold and here and there a tiny alpine lichen relieves the starkness of its barren dome. It is eight miles to the top of Half Dome, and eight miles down again!

Once you get the bacilli in your blood stream, rest assured you will be back. For there is no cure for mountain-itis except mountains; no allaying that trail-fever except by trail-trekking. And of all the treatments under the sun and the stars, there is none easier to take than that of traveling the trails of Yosemite!

The Theft of Fire
From *Miwok Myths* by Edward Winslow Gifford [*University of California Publications in American Archeology and Ethnology (1917)*, Vol. 12, No. 8.

Lizard saw the smoke. He said: "Smoking below, smoking below, smoking below, smoking below. My grandmother starts a fire to cook acorns. It is very lonely."

Flute-player (Mouse) was sent down the mountains into the valley to secure the fire. Flute-player departed, taking with him two flutes. He finally arrived at the assembly house from which the smoke was issuing. He found it crowded, but he was welcomed and the people persuaded him to play. He played and he played.

Then they put a feather mat over the smoke hole at the top of the house and shut the feathers in the door. They closed the door with the feather dress. They told the doorkeeper to close the door tight.

Flute-man played continuously. The people fell asleep and snored. Flute-player remained awake and played. Finally, he concluded that all were fast asleep. He arose and took two coals from the fire, placing them in his flute. Then he put two coals in the second flute. He proceeded to the door, cut loose the feathers, passed out, and started homeward.

The people awoke to find him gone and with him the fire. Hail and Rain were sent in pursuit, for they were the two swiftest travellers among the valley people. Hail went, but Flute-man heard Hail and Rain coming, so he threw one of his flutes under a buckeye tree. Rain asked him what he had done with the fire. "You stole our fire," Rain said. Flute-player denied it. Then Rain returned home. The placing of the flute, with the coals in it, under the buckeye tree resulted in the fire always being in the buckeye.

When Rain started back, Flute-man took his fire from under the buckeye and again proceeded homeward. He arrived at home safely and brought the fire into the assembly house. He told the people that Rain had taken one flute with coals in it. He said, "Rain took one flute from me. I have only one left."

The chief told Flute-player to build a fire, and the latter produced the coals from his remaining flute. A large fire was made. It was then that people lost their language. Those close to the fire talked correctly. The people at the north side of the assembly house talked brokenly. Those at the south side talked altogether different; so did those at the west side and at the east side. This was because of the cold.

Coyote brought entrails and threw them on the fire, extinguishing it. The people became angry and expelled Coyote, telling him to remain outside and to eat his food raw. That is why Coyote always eats his meat uncooked.

The Yosemite

The Yosemite, by John Muir (1912) In this lyrical guide, the great naturalist sketches the wonders of Yosemite and offers suggestions for walks and hikes.

Arriving by the Panama steamer, I stopped one day in San Francisco and then inquired for the nearest way out of town. "But where do you want to go?" asked the man to whom I had applied for this important information. "To any place that is wild," I said. This reply startled him. He seemed to fear I might be crazy and therefore the sooner I was out of town the better, so he directed me to the Oakland ferry.

So on the first of April, 1868, I set out afoot for Yosemite.

"Anywhere that's wild!" John Muir declared.

The Beauty of Rainbows

The Bridal Veil and Vernal Falls are famous for their rainbows; and special visits to them are often made when the sun shines into the spray at the most favorable angle. But amid the spray and foam and fine-ground mist ever rising from the various falls and cataracts there is an affluence and variety of iris bows scarcely known to visitors who stay only a day or two. Both day and night, winter and summer, this divine light may be seen wherever water is falling dancing, singing; telling the heart-peace of Nature amid the wildest displays of her power. In the bright spring mornings the black-walled recess at the foot of the Lower Yosemite Fall is lavishly fine with irised spray; and not simply does this span the dashing foam, but the foam itself, the whole mass of it, beheld at a certain distance, seems to be colored, and drips and wavers from color to color, mingling with the foliage of the adjacent trees, without suggesting any relationship to the ordinary rainbow. This is perhaps the largest and most reservoir-like fountain of iris colors to be found in the Valley.

Lunar rainbows or spray-bows also abound in the glorious affluence of dashing, rejoicing, hurrahing, enthusiastic spring floods, their colors as distinct as those of the sun and regularly and obviously banded, though less vivid. Fine specimens may be found any night at the foot of the Upper Yosemite Fall, glowing gloriously lid the gloomy shadows and thundering waters, whenever there is plenty of moonlight and spray. Even the secondary bow is at times distinctly visible.

The best point from which to observe them is on Fern Ledge. For some time after moonrise, at time of high water, the arc has a span of about five hundred feet, and is set upright; one end planted in the boiling spray at the bottom, the other in the edge of the fall, creeping lower, of course, and becoming less upright as the moon rises higher. This grand arc of color, glowing in mild, shapely beauty in so weird and huge a chamber of night shadows, and amid the rush and roar and tumultuous dashing of this thunder-voiced fall, is one of the most impressive and most cheering of all the blessed mountain evangels.

Smaller bows may be seen in the gorge on the plateau between the Upper and Lower Falls. Once toward midnight, after spending a few hours with the wild beauty of the Upper Fall, I sauntered along the edge of the gorge, looking in here and there, wherever the footing felt safe, to see what I could learn of the night aspects of the smaller falls that dwell there. And down in an exceedingly black, pit-like portion of the gorge, at the foot of the highest of the intermediate falls, into which the moonbeams were pouring through a narrow opening, I saw a well-defined spray-bow, beautifully distinct in colors, spanning the pit from side to side, while pure white foam-waves beneath the beautiful bow were constantly springing up out of the dark into the moonlight like dancing ghosts.

Yosemite Trails

Chapter VIII, The Forests of the Yosemite Region from *Yosemite Trails* (1911) by J. Smeaton Chase. This trenchant observer of trees and superb nature writer should be re-discovered!

In the valley itself the timber, fine as it is, is an incidental adornment, a feature subordinate to cliffs and waterfalls. When one is sightseeing the mind naturally focuses upon the principal objects, and takes no account of accessories, beyond observing, perhaps, that they obstruct the view. But a forest is not a sight, and the forest frame of mind is not a wide-eyed-wondering frame of mind, but is made up of innumerable small and quiet sensations, incidents, and reminiscences. Its glades and Blooms, its trees and flowers, its stealing airs and rivulets, even its sounds, are the ingredients of a calm and peaceful mood; and whenever I find myself leaving the great valley, with its varied wonders and beauties, and entering the unmixed forest, I experience a feeling of comforting ease, and relax like a man returning home at evening to walk in his garden. I know all these things and like them; and I feel that they know and like me too.

I suppose this sensation, which no doubt many people experience, might be traced to a scientific psychological source. Be that as it may, every good man loves the woodland, and even if our concerns keep us all our lives out of our heritage, we hope to lie down at last under the quiet benediction of slow-moving branches.

The regularity with which the various species of conifer appear at certain altitudes is a matter of unfailing interest to the tree-lover. Species succeeds species in orderly procession, each of them marked by special beauties, and all merging harmoniously like the colors of the spectrum.

At the lower limit of the pine-belt comes the digger pine [gray pine, foothill pine].

It is always to me a somewhat uncomfortable and unpine-like tree, more suggestive of the arid Australian flora than of our lusty occidental types. In shape it is loose and spindling, and the foliage, though long and well-tempered, is so sparse as to give the tree almost a (lying appearance. The straggling branches have a thin-blooded look, and cast a grey, anemic shade t hat scarcely mitigates the stroke of the California sun. In comparison with the sturdy vigor of the family it is just what one might expect to find on the torrid foothill slopes which it mainly inhabits, where vitality is drained away by a sun of semi-desert power, and the rainfall is barely sufficient to support tree-life.

Yet it has a pallid grace of its own, and the languid, transparent shapes impart an individual character to the landscape, somewhat akin to that which the yucca palm gives to the Mojave region. The handsome oval cones are only exceeded in size by those of Pinus coulteri and Pinus lambertiana, and contain edible nuts that provide the Indians of the locality with a relief from the overworked acorn. In the aggressive tusks which guard them we seem to see the beginning of the quarrelsome traits that mark the purely desert growths.

Next in order appears the pine which preponderates on the floor of the Yosemite Valley, the yellow pine. It begins at about two thousand feet of elevation, and continues in its common form up to about five thousand feet. This type exhibits the pine characteristics of symmetry and shapeliness at their best.

Joseph Smeaton Chase had the same publisher as John Muir and his "Yosemite Trails" got great reviews.

No other tree is so perfect in its slender tapering form, and it keeps this perfection remarkably even in old age. The bark, of a dull huffy color, is arranged in large irregular plates like alligator skin; the foliage is long and of a brilliant dark green, growing in fine star-like bursts that well indicate the vigor of the species. The lower main branches of old trees are particularly picturesque, reaching outward and downward in lines that are at once graceful and elastic, and full of fine Japanese drawing.

Overlapping the common yellow pine in some places but not everywhere, comes what may be called a mountain type of the same species, known as the Jeffrey variety. It is usually of less height but greater spread of limbs, with redder and more broken bark and much larger cones. This versatile and adventurous pine inhabits a wide range of altitude, and has a way of turning up in all manner of unlikely places.. On wind-swept granite pavements, which the trees proper to the altitude decline with thanks, there the Jeffrey appears, takes a wrestler's grip, and holds on like a bull-dog. One of these trees has rooted itself on the topmost round of the Sentinel Dome, and there romps joyously about in the terrific wind that rushes continually over that exposed spot, its branches and foliage streaming out horizontally like a stormy oriflamme of war.

On the long promontories that stretch out into the Mono plains on the eastern side of the Sierra, this brave pine marches out green and sturdy among the bleached and wizened desert growths. Wherever you find it, it is always heartening and cheerful in bearing, an entire contrast to the misanthropical juniper that often grows with it. The one chooses the starkest places because they suit its own dour temper; the other out of pure *joie de vivre* and love of fighting.

The juniper (juniperus occidentalis) is a kind of churlish relative of the conifers, entirely unlike them and opposed in every line and instinct to their aspiring characteristics. For purposes of contrast, nothing could be better than this squat, Japanese-wrestler looking tree, which one encounters growing in the most difficult and uncomfortable places at all elevations from six thousand to ten thousand feet.

Wherever storms career most wildly, and on glacial pavements and ledges of the most uncompromising granite where nothing else beside lichens and mosses cares to grow, there this embittered tree exists,—it cannot he said to flourish,—and hugs itself into a morose longevity, like a miser living to a hundred on crusts. High up on wind-swept angles of mountain you may see them peering and leering down at you, their stumpy trunks twisted into alarming contortions.

Death Valley NP
Lava Beds NM
Yosemite National Park
Joshua Tree National Park
Pinnacles NP
Eugene O'Neill NHS
Muir Woods NM
Whiskeytown-Shasta Trinity NRA
Golden Gate National Recreation Area
Redwood NP
Channel Islands National Park
Devils Postpile NM
Lassen Volcanic National Park
Cabrillo NM
Mojave NPRES
César Chávez NM
John Muir NHS
Rosie the Riveter NHS
Santa Monica Mountains NRA
Point Reyes NS
Sequoia-Kings Canyon National Parks

California's National Parks

Other states have national parks with tall trees, high peaks, deep canyons, long seashores and vast deserts, but only California can claim all these grand landscapes within its boundaries.

California boasts nine national parks, the most in the nation. In addition, the state's national parklands include national recreation areas, national monuments, national historic parks, a national seashore and a national preserve.

The state features one of America's oldest national parks—Yosemite set aside in 1890—and one of its newest—César E. Chávez National Monument established in 2012.

Mere acreage does not a national park make, but California's national parks include the largest park in the contiguous U.S.—3.3-million acre Death Valley National Park. Yosemite (748,542 acres) and Joshua Tree (790,636 acres) are also huge by any park standards. Even such smaller parklands as Redwoods National Park and Pt. Reyes National Seashore are by no means small.

California and The National Park Idea

Not long after John Muir walked through Mariposa Grove and into the Yosemite Valley, California's natural treasures attracted attention worldwide and conservationists rallied to preserve them as parks. As the great naturalist put it in 1898: "Thousands of nerve-shaken, overcivilized people are beginning to find out that going to the mountains is going home; that wilderness is a necessity; and that mountain parks and reservations are useful not only as fountains of timber and irrigating rivers, but as fountains of life."

The National Park Service, founded in 1916, was initially guided by borax tycoon-turned-park-champion Stephen T. Mather and his young assistant, California attorney Horace Albright. The park service's mission was the preservation of "the scenery and the natural and historic objects and the wild life" and the provision "for the enjoyment of the same in such manner and by such means as will leave them unimpaired for the enjoyment of future generations."

The invention of the automobile revolutionized national park visitation, particularly in car-conscious California. John Muir called them "blunt-nosed mechanical beetles," yet as one California senator pointed out, "If Jesus Christ had an automobile he wouldn't have ridden a jackass into Jerusalem."

With cars came trailers, and with trailer camps came concessionaires. National parks filled with mobile cities of canvas and aluminum, and by visitors anxious to see California's natural wonders. During the 1920s and 30s, the park service constructed signs identifying scenic features and rangers assumed the role of interpreting nature for visitors.

By 1930 California had four national parks: Yosemite, Lassen, Sequoia and General Grant (Kings Canyon.) In the 1930s, two big desert areas—Joshua Tree and Death Valley—became national monuments.

With the 1960s came hotly contested, and eventually successful campaigns to create Redwood National

Steven Mather (R) and his assistant Horace Albright guided the National Park Service in its early days.

Park and Point Reyes National Seashore. During the 1970s the National Park Service established parks near the state's big cities—Golden Gate National Recreation Area on the San Francisco waterfront and Marin headlands and Santa Monica Mountains National Recreation Area, a Mediterranean ecosystem near Los Angeles. Also during that decade, Mineral King Valley was saved from a mega-ski resort development and added to Sequoia National Park. Channel Islands National Park, an archipelago offshore from Santa Barbara, was established in 1980.

During the 1980s and 1990s, major conservation battles raged in the desert. After more than two decades of wrangling, Joshua Tree and Death Valley national monuments were greatly expanded and given national park status, and the 1.6-million acre Mojave National Preserve was established under provisions of the 1994 California Desert Conservation Act.

Today, the National Park Service must address challenging questions: How best to regulate concessionaires? Should motor vehicles be banned from Yosemite Valley? How can aging park facilities cope with many years of deferred maintenance?

And the biggest issue of all: How will our parks (indeed our planet!) cope with the rapidly increasing effects of climate change?

The consequences of climate change to California's national parks is ever more apparent. In recent years, after prolonged droughts, devastating wildfires burned the Yosemite backcountry, parts of Sequoia National Park and more than half the Santa Monica Mountains National Recreation Area. Scientists have discovered that trees in Sequoia and Kings Canyon national parks endure the worst ozone levels of all national parks, in part because of their proximity to farm-belt air in the San Joaquin Valley.

California's national parklands struggle with an ever-increasing numbers of visitors. The California Office of Tourism charts visitation to national parks along with airports, hotel occupancy and other attractions such as Disneyland and Universal Studios. Yosemite is California's most-visited park with 4.5 to 5 million visitors a year, and many other parks count millions of visitors or "visitor days," per year.

What may be the saving grace of national parks is the deep-seated, multi-generational pride Americans have for their national parklands. We not only love national parks, we love the very idea of national parks. Even in an era of public mistrust toward government, national parks remain one of the most beloved institutions of American life.

National Parks have often been celebrated as America's best idea. As writer Wallace Stegner put it: "National parks are the best idea we ever had. Absolutely American, absolutely democratic, they reflect us at our best rather than our worst."

The Trails

The state of the state's national park trail system is excellent. Trailhead parking, interpretive panels and displays, as well as signage, is generally tops in the field. Backcountry junctions are usually signed and trail conditions, with a few exceptions of course, range from good to excellent.

Trail systems evolved on a park-by-park basis and it's difficult to speak in generalities about their respective origins. A good deal of Yosemite's trail system was in place before the early horseless carriages chugged into the park.

Several national parks were aided greatly by the Depression-era Civilian Conservation Corps of the 1930s. Sequoia and Pinnacles national parks, for example, have hand-built trails by the CCC that are true gems, highlighted by stonework and bridges that would no doubt be prohibitively expensive to construct today.

Scout troops, the hard-working young men and women of the California Conservation Corps and many volunteer groups are among the organizations that help park staff build and maintain trails.

The trail system in California's national parklands shares many characteristics in common with pathways overseen by other governmental bodies, and have unique qualities as well. One major difference between national parks and, for example, California's state parks, is the amount of land preserved as wilderness. A majority of Yosemite, Sequoia, Death Valley, Joshua Tree and several more parks are official federally designated wilderness. Wilderness comprises some 94 percent of Yosemite National Park, 93 percent of Death Valley National Park, and more than 80 percent of Joshua Tree National Park.

On national park maps you'll find wilderness areas delineated as simply "Wilderness." Unlike the Forest Service, the Bureau of Land Management or other wilderness stewards, the National Park Service does not name its wilderness areas.

Author John McKinney admires the sign for Yosemite's Four Mile Trail.

"Wilderness" is more than a name for a wild area. By law, a wilderness is restricted to non-motorized entry—that is to say, equestrian and foot travel. Happily, hikers do not have to share the trails with snowmobiles or mountain bikes in national park wilderness.

Because national park trails attract visitors from all over the globe, the park service makes use of international symbols on its signage, and the metric system as well. Don't be surprised if you spot trail signs with distance expressed in kilometers as well as miles and elevation noted in meters as well as feet.

The hikers you meet on a national park trail may be different from the company you keep on trails near home. California's national parks attract increasing numbers of ethnically and culturally diverse hikers of all ages, shapes and sizes, from across the nation and around the world. Once I counted ten languages on a popular trail in Yosemite! The hiking experience is much enriched by sharing the trail with hikers from literally all walks of life.

California's National Parklands

Alcatraz Island
Cabrillo National Monument
Castle Mountains National Monument
César E. Chávez National Monument
Channel Islands National Park
Death Valley National Park
Devils Postpile National Monument
Eugene O'Neill National Historic Site
Fort Point National Historic Site
Golden Gate National Recreation Area
John Muir National Historic Site
Joshua Tree National Park
Lassen Volcanic National Park
Lava Beds National Monument
Manzanar National Historic Site
Mojave National Preserve
Muir Woods National Monument
Pinnacles National Park
Point Reyes National Seashore
Port Chicago Naval Magazine National Memorial
Presidio of San Francisco
Redwood National and State Parks
Rosie the Riveter WWII Home Front National
    Historic Park
San Francisco Maritime National Historic Park
Santa Monica Mountains National Recreation Area
Sequoia and Kings Canyon National Parks
Tule Lake National Monument
Whiskeytown National Recreation Area
Yosemite National Park

HIKE Yosemite

The Hiker's Index

Celebrating the Scenic, Sublime and Sensational Points of Interest in California's National Parks

State with the most National Parks
California, with 9

Largest National Park in Contiguous U.S.
Death Valley with 3.3 million acres

Third Largest National Park in Contiguous U.S.
Mojave National Preserve

Foggiest Place on the West Coast
Point Reyes Lighthouse, Point Reyes National Seashore

World's Tallest Tree
A 379.7-foot high coast redwood named Hyperion in Redwood National Park

World's Largest Tree
General Sherman Tree, 275 feet tall, with a base circumference of 102 feet, growing in the Giant Forest Area of Sequoia National Park

World's Largest-In-Diameter Tree

General Grant Tree, dubbed "the nation's Christmas tree," more than 40 feet in diameter at its base, growing in Kings Canyon National Park.

Largest Elephant Seal Population on Earth

San Miguel Island, Channel Islands National Park

Highest Point in Contiguous U.S.

Mt. Whitney (14,508 feet in elevation) on the far eastern boundary of Sequoia National Park

Lowest Point in Western Hemisphere

Badwater (282 feet below sea level) in Death Valley National Park

California's Largest Island

Santa Cruz Island, Channel Islands National Park

Only Major Metropolis Bisected by a Mountain Range

Los Angeles, by the Santa Monica Mountains (National Recreation Area)

Highest Waterfall in North America

Yosemite Falls, at 2,425 feet, in Yosemite National Park

JOHN MCKINNEY

John McKinney is an award-winning writer, public speaker, and author of 30 hiking-themed books: inspiring narratives, top-selling guides, books for children.

John is particularly passionate about sharing the stories of California trails. He is the only one to have visited—and written about—all 280 California State Parks. John tells the story of his epic hike along the entire California coast in the critically acclaimed *Hiking on the Edge: Dreams, Schemes, and 1600 Miles on the California Coastal Trail*.

For 18 years John, aka The Trailmaster, wrote a weekly hiking column for the Los Angeles Times, and has hiked and enthusiastically told the story of more than 10 thousand miles of trail across California and around the world. His "Every Trail Tells a Story" series of guides highlight the very best hikes in California.

The intrepid Eagle Scout has written more than a thousand stories and opinion pieces about hiking, parklands, and our relationship with nature.

A passionate advocate for hiking and our need to reconnect with nature, John is a frequent public speaker, and shares his tales on radio, on video, and online.

JOHN MCKINNEY:
"EVERY TRAIL TELLS A STORY."

Hike On.

TheTrailmaster.com

www.ingramcontent.com/pod-product-compliance
Lightning Source LLC
Chambersburg PA
CBHW032042290426
44110CB00012B/909